A NIGHT OUT WITH
ROBERT BURNS

A NIGHT OUT WITH
ROBERT BURNS

The Greatest Poems

Arranged by
Andrew O'Hagan

CANONGATE

Edinburgh · London · New York · Melbourne

This edition first published in Great Britain in 2008 by
Canongate Books Ltd, 14 High Street
Edinburgh EH1 1TE

1

**Scottish
Arts** Council

The publishers gratefully acknowledge subsidy from the Scottish Arts Council
towards the publication of this title

British Library Cataloguing-in-Publication Data
A catalogue record for this book is available on
request from the British Library

ISBN 978 1 84195 992 4

Typeset by Palimpsest Book Production Ltd, Grangemouth, Stirlingshire

Printed and bound in Great Britain by Mackays of Chatham plc. Chatham, Kent
www.canongate.net

Contents

In memory of Larry Rhodes
(1967–2002)

A Birl for Burns

From the start, Burns' birl and rhythm,
That tongue the Ulster Scots brought wi' them
And stick to still in County Antrim
    Was in my ear.
From east of Bann it westered in
    On the Derry air.

My neighbours *toved* and *bummed* and *blowed*,
They *happed* themselves until it *thowed*,
By *slaps* and *stiles* they *thrawed* and *tholed*
    And *snedded thrissles,*
And when the rigs were *braked* and hoed
    They'd *wet their whistles.*

Old men and women getting crabbèd
Would hark like dogs who'd seen a rabbit,
Then straighten, stare and have a stab at
    Standard habbie:
Custom never staled their habit
    O' quotin' Rabbie.

Leg-lifting, heartsome, lightsome Burns!
He overflowed the well-wrought urns
Like buttermilk from slurping churns,
    Rich and unruly,
Or dancers flying, doing turns
    At some wild hooley.

For Rabbie's free and Rabbie's big,
His stanza may be tight and trig
But once he sets the sail and rig
   Away he goes
Like Tam-O-Shanter o'er the brig
   Where no one follows.

And though his first tongue's going, gone,
And word lists now get added on
And even words like *stroan* and *thrawn*
   Have to be glossed,
In Burns's rhymes they travel on
   And won't be lost.

                    Seamus Heaney

Introduction

They say the rain fell heavily that day. It was 25 January 1820 and Alexander Boswell — son of the more famous James — bent down to lay the foundation stone of what would become the Burns Monument, erected in Alloway near where the poet was born. From Carrick Hill, where the stone figure of Burns stands enclosed in Gothic ornament, you can see for many miles — over fields, rivers and bridges to the hearts of those towns that can track their life-blood in Burns's poems.

'There surely lives,' said Alexander Boswell, 'no man so dull, so flinty, or phlegmatic, who could witness this event without emotion. But to those whose heart-strings have thrilled responsive to the poet's lyre — whose bosoms have swelled like his, with love and friendship, with tenderness and sympathy, have glowed with patriotism or panted for glory — this hour must be an hour of exultation.'

But Alexander's tears, like those of a number of his contemporaries, must have been slightly salted with guilt, for few poets — even of the Romantic breed — had been allowed to die quite as penniless as Burns. The well-to-do of Edinburgh had lionised him for a season then dropped him like a sack of Ayrshire potatoes. One of his friends said that for every smart remark that came out of Burns's mouth, he made a hundred enemies.

It took nearly two dozen years to raise the money for the Alloway monument, and even then the subscription was short. Thomas Carlyle put the matter bluntly:

It was a curious phenomenon, in the withered, unbelieving, second-hand 18th century, that of a Hero, starting up, among the artificial paste-board figures and productions, in the guise of a Robert Burns. Perhaps no man had such a false reception from his fellow men. You would think it strange if I called Burns the most gifted British soul we had in all that century of his: and yet I believe the day is coming when there will be little danger in saying so.

I once went in search of the Burns who mattered to people. It was a good few winters ago, and rain had frozen to snow, which lay thick on the ground of Alloway the day I arrived. The driver could hardly see anything; every few miles he stepped out to scrape the frost from the windscreen. The light was going – 'dim-dark'ning thro' the flaky show'r / Or whirling drift' – and for a moment, but for the car, it seemed we could be in any century.

The whole of Alloway is now more or less given over to something called the Burns National Heritage Park. This includes Burns Cottage (the birthplace), plus a museum full of manuscripts and memorabilia (and toffee). It also includes the Old Alloway Kirk (where Burns's father is buried), the Burns Monument and a new building which houses the Tam o' Shanter Experience.

However grim the Burns family cottage was in 1759, it could hardly be any worse than it is now. You go in wearing earphones, and it's freezing and dark as you sit down to watch one of those heritage flicks full of Scottish sunsets and ruddy-cheeked people. The room where the Burns family sat together is cold and Calvinist: no crack of light or laughter there. Wooden dolls stand around a table, being taught all the good ways by a bigger doll in the shape of Burns's father.

The museum has some good first editions. The manuscripts of correspondence offer a lively view of Burns's life on earth. You see relics of his early education: a Bible and a book of English essayists; bits of French and Latin, evidence of good relations with a young local teacher, John Murdoch, who considered Robert and his brother Gilbert to 'have no ear for music'. Then there are artefacts relating to the life of a young man, a romancer and a hard worker: his razor and shaving mirror, his drinking vessels, his pendants, his pens and proof of their various productions.

As you look over these bits and bobs, a motion picture of Burns's life begins to roll. Born in that barn outside the museum, it was no time at all before the young Robert went wandering by the River Afton with his finger on his chin. The family moved to Mount Oliphant farm – not far away – when he was seven. An indication of the way things were to be came when Robert spied a blacksmith's daughter, Nellie Kilpatrick, and wrote a poem about how she'd captured his heart. His walks through Ayrshire brought further poems, chiefly about the things that caught his eye, and chiefly in the Scottish dialect.

He joined a dancing class at Tarbolton (to meet girls); he formed the Bachelors' Club (to meet his pals); he became a Freemason; and he tried to learn the trade of flax-dressing at Irvine, ten miles along the coast. Tales of affairs follow: girls getting pregnant; advances sought and sometimes rebuffed; troubles with the Kirk because of all his carry-on. We hear of his plans for emigration to Jamaica; his attempts to marry Jean Armour and his repudiation by her father; his loss of the adored Highland Mary, who may have died in child-birth; his shelving of the Jamaica plans; and his triumphant debut with the *Kilmarnock Poems*. Burns's life actually unfolds more like an opera than a film – no wonder Gene Kelly's ambition was to make a musical of it.

Burns made it in Edinburgh, where he'd gone on a borrowed donkey, but ventured home to poverty a few months later. He took a lease on a hopeless farm called Ellisland; he became an exciseman; his wife had more children, and so did women who were not his wife (Mrs Burns said that 'Our Robin shoulda hud twa wives.') He started collecting old Scots songs, and rewriting many of them, for publication; he fell in and out with friends; he fell foul of gossip-mongers and idiots, who ruined his chances of advancement in the Excise; he dissipated a bit, though probably not as much as people said at the time. He liked a drink. He had a bad heart – a mental case of a doctor thought to cure it by having him wade in the Solway Firth. But he died, aged 37, in a house up a scabby lane in Dumfries. He was feverish and ravaged, his heart was in bits, and there was hardly a penny in the house.

This is a little of what we know about Robert Burns. The episodes are like scenes in an overblown drama, and each is captured in the portraits and pocketbooks that stood around me in the Burns Museum. Out in the foyer were many of the productions of Burns's incredible afterlife: shortbread and haggis, tea-towels and trays, happy notepads and dodgy tapes. Everything for everybody, or nothing for nobody, depending on where you sit. The 'Burns cult' that so annoyed Hugh MacDiarmid finds its primary – though quite harmless – expression in this gallery of trinkets and toffees. They are testament to how successful a brand name and face Burns has become. The shop sells the books as well, and collections of letters and lives. The other stuff is just tourism: people want to show they've been somewhere, even if they haven't been anywhere yet.

I had the Tam o' Shanter Experience on my own, bar one other person. It was a fairly big auditorium, well decorated with trees and atmospheric bits and pieces around the sides. The screen was split into three. Tam appeared in the middle panel, getting 'fou and unco happy', and then the remaining screens were filled with the other characters in the tale as it unfolded. It was riveting, and I only wished there were some kids around to squeal and whoop and hide their faces as Tam gets involved with the witches.

A lot of the butchers and bakers in and around Ayrshire have the well-known Nasmyth portrait stuck to their shop windows, the way some cafés and grocers used to have the Queen, and some Italian delis still have the Pope. I wondered if it said something more than that, something like: 'We sell haggis and shortbread in here.' Ayr is one of those towns that likes to make its traditions a big part of the here and now. You can read your way from one end of the place to the other. Over here is the Brigate – the 'path to the bridge' – which signifies that there must be a river down there; and over here is Kirkgate, the 'path to the church'. Even if the bridge and the church no longer exist, you know that they once did because of the words that remain.

In Ayr I was looking for an address in the Sandgate, so I started walking towards the harbour and the shore. You imagine that you can smell the oily water and taste something of the salt. The man I wanted to speak to, Robin Jenkins, was in the makeshift Burns Festival offices. He worked for a government-sponsored agency called Enterprise Ayrshire, and the two outfits saw their objectives as being very much related. He was a big man, with big ideas that immediately seemed not unrelated to the bigness of his handshake. The Sandgate offices were chaotic: boxes of leaflets and publicity hand outs were stacked everywhere; calls were coming in from around the world, calls from people interested in coming over to the Land o' Burns, taking part in the festivities, spending their money. John Struthers, the festival organiser, was walking briskly back and forth across the main office – sorting things, advising the telephonists, trying to get the national poet's anniversary do into full swing.

I asked Mr Jenkins what they were all trying to achieve through Robert Burns. 'In marketing terms,' he said, 'you're always looking for a unique selling point, a unique proposition. The south-west of Scotland is the only area in the world which has this connection with Burns. If you look at what he actually did in his lifetime – I think it's fair to say that "Auld Lang Syne" is the second most popular song after "Happy Birthday" – you see he is a very attractive product. People come to visit this area for golf, for castles and for Robert Burns.' Robin Jenkins knew his business, and he referred to Burns as a 'product' (and Ayrshire as an 'opportunity') in a completely unselfconscious way. I wondered whether it wasn't a bit desperate to focus so much on tourism, on the servicing of passers-by. Wasn't it a shoddy replacement for investment in real industry? 'I refute that,' he said. 'There are a lot of plus points in what we're doing.

We invested in Prestwick Airport, in local manufacturing and development. We want to get our product right. Today, in fact, our executive and some of our directors have flown down for a major promotional push in London. We want to make sure a lot of the people in the City are aware of Ayrshire as a major place to live, work and play in.'

The executives of Enterprise Ayrshire were trying to think of ways to make a success of the Burns initiative. They planned something called a Taste of Burns Country: 45 local companies would be marketed as producers and caterers of fine food at reasonable prices. Robin Jenkins said they were keen not to despoil Burns's message by linking it to the wrong products. Crawfords – the biscuit people – had asked if they could use the official Burns Festival logo on their new shortbread tin. The answer was yes. Safeway wanted to use the logo throughout their stores – and that was OK as well. Manufacturers of cheap scarves or useless pens, though, would not be allowed to brand their goods.

I asked Mr Jenkins how the marketing of Burns compared with the pushing of a theme park or a golf course. 'Burns is a lot easier,' he said, 'because there's a human interest aspect to him. I hadn't realised until I looked at some of the booklets and information on Burns how much he was almost ahead of his time. I mean, at the World Travel Market, we had this initiative where we promoted Ayrshire, Dumfries and Galloway together. I came across a phrase in one of his poems that said, "Welcome, welcome again", and that just captures exactly what we're trying to do. People are welcome to come here, so long as they come again and again. I don't see any conflict in the use of that – so long as it's done in the best possible taste.'

Is there something special about Burns, that he so lends himself to commercial enterprise of this kind? The only rival would be Stratford-upon-Avon and its relationship with Shakespeare. Thomas Hardy inspires no such turnover in the land he called Wessex. Even in America – where Whitman-furters, the Emily Dickinson Matchstick Doll's House and the Emersonian Nature Kit would not seem terribly out of place – there is nothing really to compare with the Burns trademark. There is no Twainworld to speak of, no Hawthorne Haunted House, or Ahab's Universe of Water. Burns did give imaginative life to the towns of Ayrshire, Dumfries and Galloway; he did, with quite unbelievable felicity, characterise the familiars of his time and place – those farmers, doctors, ministers, taxmen, peasant lassies and lairds – and he did exhibit extraordinary sympathy for nature, and a genius for understanding the way its productions relate to human feeling and for the special modes of expression in late 18th-century lowland Scotland. Who else could make so much of a mouse, and with so spectacular a result?

> That wee-bit heap o' leaves an' stibble,
> Has cost thee monie a weary nibble!
> Now thou's turn'd out, for a' thy trouble,
> But house or hald,
> To thole the Winter's *sleety dribble*,
> An' *cranreuch* cauld!

> But Mousie, thou art no thy-lane,
> In proving *foresight* may be vain:
> The best laid schemes o' *Mice* an' *Men*,
> Gang aft agley,
> An' lea'e us nought but grief an' pain,
> For promis'd joy!

> Still, thou art blest, compared wi' *me*!
> The *present* only toucheth thee:
> But Och! I *backward* cast my e'e,
> On prospects drear!
> An' *forward*, tho' I canna *see*,
> I *guess* an' *fear*!

Burns was a satirist of the first water. No religious piety, no political hypocrisy, no brand of inhumanity or inequality, no cheerless idiocy or tactless ambition – even those he could claim as his own – remained as it had been after the best of his poetry. But these are qualities that exceptional people might have, that artists might deploy to the clamour of fame, and though it is very unusual for one person to carry so much newness in themselves, so much variety, and so to embody a tradition as well, it is not unprecedented. Even in that century of his – the century so derided by Carlyle, over which Burns was seen to stride like a colossus – several great persons stood in the way of Robert Burns's claim to the prize. So his genius alone will not explain the extent of his marketability, the sheer number and variety of mugs and tea-towels on which his face appears.

It may be that Burns's sort of fame (his sort of usefulness) depends on selective memory, on selective understanding, and certainly on selective reading. He is the dream advertising tool not because of his localness, or because he is sexually and politically explosive, or because he is difficult and strange, but because he is pure and direct. He is the ideal marketing tool because he can be all of these things, while seeming to be nothing too particular. Burns can seem to be universal. He can seem a pure lover, a pure worker, a pure patriot, a pure loyalist, a pure man of nature wherever it may occur. He can seem to mean nothing, and only to feel. He knew this himself: it could, in fact, be argued that it was Burns who began the process of turning himself into an 'easy listening' poet. He knew that a selective rendering of his life, his habits and his work would do him no harm with the well-to-do. The poems stood for themselves, but Burns gave us hints about how to appreciate him, and make use of him, without having to deal with the troublesome edge of many of his poems, letters and songs. He hid himself especially well. Those songs might sound an antique note of beauty, but many of them also make a political noise. The memory of Culloden may be a hammerless bell now, but in 1790, when Burns 'discovered' the following air, it had more of the character of an alarm:

By yon castle wa' at the close of the day,
I heard a man sing tho' his head it was grey;
And as he was singing, the tears down came,
There'll never be peace till Jamie comes hame.—
The Church is in ruins, the State is in jars,
Delusions, oppressions, and murderous wars:
We dare na weel say't, but we ken wha's to blame,
There'll never be peace till Jamie comes hame.—

My seven braw sons for Jamie drew sword,
And now I greet round their green beds in the yerd;
It brak the sweet heart of my faithfu' auld Dame,
There'll never be peace till Jamie comes hame.—
Now life is a burden that bows me down,
Sin I tint my bairns, and he tint his crown;
But till my last moments my words are the same,
There'll never be peace till Jamie comes hame.—

He framed himself as a rustic, a loveable rogue, a universal singer of nature, a blithe and unspecific defender of human rights. We can see why he did it – for preferment and an easier life – and we might love him nonetheless. But it may draw us closer to our question, if not yet to our answer: why is Burns so easy to market to the world? Burns has been harnessed now, like no one else, to represent the romantic spirit of the common man, and there are common men the world over who are keen to hear him. He may have been taken out of his time, the bite of his satire may leave no mark, but he is now an icon for strong general feelings, universally understood: he is perpetually at one with the stars, in love with little mice, swelling to the noise of rivers, the flush on a young girl's cheek, outraged and saddened at poverty. The world – and his own little world of Ayrshire knows the benefits – has followed his own impulse towards self-immortalisation; it has made him somebody by seeing him as nobody; it has sought to make a place for him as a Man of Men, and his signature tune 'A Man's a Man for A'That' has become a sort of 'Marseillaise' for the world. 'Auld Lang Syne' as 'Happy Birthday'.

There are now two classes of people who recognise the name Robert Burns: those who think he has lovely things to say about daisies, and those who seek to bring out the troubled wisdom of his work, to rescue it, and let it do its damage in these damaged times. There are two audiences for Burns: those who wonder about the extent of his sympathy for the French Revolution, and those who want a few bonnie words on a plate to put on their kitchen wall. It is very unusual. These two groups are often at odds over Burns, but they share a powerful set of sentiments about this ghost of a national poet, in that ghost of a nation.

Burns's friend David Sillar is buried behind Irvine Old Parish Church. He died long after Burns, who had written about him, and to him, encouraging Sillar's interest in poetry and the fiddle. Irvine is hard against the Ayrshire coast; Sillar ran a nautical school here in the early 1800s, and was one of the founders of the Irvine Burns Club. Burns's lines on Sillar hung about the graveyard the Sunday morning I joined the service. There's some dispute as to whether Burns actually wrote them, but here they are:

> Should a' be true the prophets tell,
> If I the lines am fit to spell,
> King David mair o' dirt should smell
> Than Deity,
> And gin there's sic a place as Hell—
> Look up and see!

Inside the kirk, light streamed in at the windows. Intimations on the reverse side of the Order of Service told me that 'the soup lunch scheduled for today has been cancelled'. They also informed me that the speakers at the Women's Guild meeting on Monday evening would be G. and A. Murray, on the topic of China Restoration. While a great deal has changed around Irvine's Old Kirk in the last two hundred years – the widening of the harbour and the new trade links associated with that; the more recent building of high flats, shopping malls and all the shapely accoutrements of a New Town – much in this little walled-off churchyard hasn't changed at all. There are Scottish continuities about the place, and it is visited by people whose faces, whose voices, whose habits too, bear the heavy stamp of ancestors who filled these pews, or ones very like them, though certainly they did so in greater numbers.

The minister wore a radio microphone. As he fixed it on, I realised how often it had occurred to me that the real difference between the churches of Catholics and those of Protestants – in Scotland at least – lies in their varying attitudes towards sound, colour and smell. The Catholic priest will whisper invitingly to an audience of secret whisperers; the Kirk minister will bellow from the pulpit and look for a raising of voices in song. The priest wears robes of lurid colours, surrounds himself with flowers and coloured marble, and clutches his golden bowls; the minister wears black, and his church is all dark hues. The Catholic chapel is filled with the smell of incense and candle wax, the whiff of corked wine; in the Kirk of Scotland you smell books. For many of us – those now lost to the cares of reformation and orthodoxy – the old battle is not one that draws on the passions so much as the senses.

Irvine's minister adjusted his mike again, and stepped down from the pulpit to greet us. This was a service in memory of Robert Burns. The reverend held up a small wooden stool and asked if anybody had one of them at home. He asked what it was for, and a little girl shouted: 'To sit on when you're bad.' She was right. It was a 'cutty stool' of the kind used to punish sinners in Burns's time – in this kirk and in kirks all over Ayrshire – and Burns himself was made to sit on it several times, usually for the sin of fornication. The congregation was asked to repeat the First Commandment over and over: 'Thou shalt have no other gods before me.' Moving between Scots and standard English, the minister wondered aloud what Burns would say to us now if he were sitting at our side. He'd notice they'd taken the old bridge away, replaced it with a shopping precinct, a 'tin box', on either side of which were churches that now stood empty and dilapidated. (He spoke in the 'voice' of Burns.) 'Whit aboot drugs,' he said, 'an epidemic that is set to ruin us?' The minister made his way through the social evils of today, and wound up having Burns say that he'd rather be in his own time, with the rules of his own day, than be stuck here with us now.

A man stood up in the pulpit to give a reading. He had been my Classics teacher at school. He was greyer now, and he wore the glittering chains that denoted his office: president of the Irvine Burns Club. I'd not known he was a Burns man when I was messing about in his classroom a dozen years before. I couldn't help wishing I'd listened to him more. In that terrible way you do from time to time, I realised I'd probably got the wrong end of the man; my certainties about everything then had been the fickle and immoderate certainties of a child. He seemed a decent sort of bloke to me now: no authoritarian ogre, no hard case, no wiseacre. Maybe I was getting old already; my sense, as I watched my former teacher speak, was not really of regret or anything like that, but of serenity. He seemed to me just someone with a life of his own, someone with interests that I shared. But the sight of him made me think of a legion of boys and girls I'd run with at school and never seen again, except in the bright colours of memory.

On that Burns memorial day, my feelings were already swelling with a Burnsian sense of things gone and done, times past, life lived. I felt I'd momentarily come close to the heart of Burns's appeal: his works are brilliant evocations of time and place – for some, of all times and all places – and he had a genius for helping us to feel sorry for ourselves. I'd come here to think about Burns's satires on the church, on intolerance, on piety, but, as on many occasions involving this odd national figure, I'd quickly been drawn towards the pathetic, towards things that got me thinking on auld lang syne. As my old teacher came to the end of his reading, and my mental pictures of his former pupils escaped out of the glorious high windows of the kirk, a fiddler struck up 'John Anderson My Jo', and I knew I'd arrived in Burns's duplicitous, delightful, shameful, essential world of golden sentiment:

> John Anderson my jo, John,
>   We clamb the hill the gither;
> And mony a canty day, John,
>   We've had wi' ane anither:
> Now we maun totter down, John,
>   And hand in hand we'll go;
> And sleep the gither at the foot,
>   John Anderson my Jo.

The year I looked for the story of Burns in the present day, I sat with the scholar Patrick Scott Hogg in a waiting-room attached to the ferry terminal at Stranraer. The snow outside wasn't a joke any more. It was vicious: the sea was in a roar. I'm sure he wouldn't care for you to say so, but the most immediately striking thing about Hogg was how much he looked like Robert Burns. When I saw him – and after having felt what I felt about the similar looks of old farmers and old writers with a passion for Burns – I suspected there might be some devil at work. But no: Mr Hogg is clear-eyed and sideboarded, his hair is brown and thick, an inch or so longer and it would be fit to be tied, just like the poet's. A bank of video games torpedoed and yelped at our backs as we sat talking. I asked him about his mother and father. 'My father was a fisherman,' he said. 'He used to take us in his boat around the cliffs of Galloway. He was a hard, tough old guy, you know, and quite hard on us.' I wondered if his father had a feeling for poetry. 'There was a certain amount of suppression there, but my grandfather played the bagpipes; there was always music around us. There was always a family yarn about us being related to James Hogg, the Ettrick Shepherd, but he only had daughters so far as I know. My mother came from a big agricultural family in this area. There was music there too.'

Scott Hogg's was one of those childhoods spent trying to find ways to enlarge himself. He read philosophy, and was forever trying to get his hands on books. He went to Stirling University, but he fell out with an academic over some point of interpretation in D.H. Lawrence and left. He said he'd always wanted to be a writer, but he'd never really had the liberty. He'd planned a novel when he was 18, an ambitious thing about the great poets meeting on a mountain, to be called 'Parnassus Awaiting'. He didn't get on with it. 'I'm working on one now,' he told me. 'I'd like to do for the area around here, around Galloway, what Lewis Grassic Gibbon did for the Mearns. It's about independent, stubborn men who have hard lives but are intelligent human beings.'

His work on Burns came about through his love of where he lives, and his hatred of sentimentality. 'I'm a single-minded swine,' he said. Patrick Scott Hogg is one of those men you find around the worlds of Burns – around the worlds of poetry generally – who, for good and decent reasons, want to have their say, and want to speak about common things. He is under the influence of the commoners' poet par excellence. Scott Hogg had been on the dole for a while, and had a wife and two children. The whole thing seemed to have become a mission for him. 'I just noticed one day,' he said, 'that the common picture of Burns didn't match the picture I had in my head of what the guy was about. He came from a working background, he had to work his bollocks off. It was a hard, tough life. All that sentimental stuff, to any thinking person, is just a myth. He had a rationalised, holistic view of the moral world. He tried to rationalise his own time – and there's loads of us who'd like to do the same thing now.' He had a strong sense that the sting had been taken out of Burns: the political message had been diluted or erased; the power of the poetry and its relevance for modern times had been diminished; and the annual celebrations of Burns had become pantomimic.

He decided to write a book called 'The Patriot Bard', and it was during his research, as he looked through numbers of the *Morning*

Chronicle and other radical papers of the 1790s, that he found what he believes are previously unattributed poems by Burns. The poems I've seen are more or less bad, but Burns is not famous for never having written a bad poem. They are certainly radical. Burns's politics are all over the place: he could support the French Revolution, but also rewrite Jacobite songs about the restoration of the Stuart king. He could join in songs and slanders against the Hanoverians while working as a civil servant and writing letters to his superiors saluting all that was Britishly royalist, though probably he did this for fear of his livelihood. But the sentiments of the new poems are not beyond him; nor is their lack of felicity. It has long been known that he had a connection with the paper, and he promised them stuff if a safe conduit could be established. One writer about Burns, Dr Andrew Noble, has made a persuasive point: 'Even if the poems are not by Robert Burns — and there are good reasons to think they might be – then they are by a very interesting, brilliant individual, writing potentially seditious material, in imitation of Burns, at a time when Burns was known to be working for the Excise. Burns was a civil servant. He could have been executed for treason if these poems were found to be his. It has incredible implications for our understanding of Burns, or for the literary and political culture of Scotland at the close of the 18th century, or perhaps for both.' Patrick Scott Hogg leaned across the Formica: 'These people who just want to keep Burns cosy,' he said, 'they are his jailers. They have political reasons of their own for trying to keep him safe and harmless and sentimental.'

The Kilwinning Mother Lodge (No. 0) was having its Burns Supper a few weeks later. All present and former members of the club – including Alexander Boswell, who eventually lost his life in a duel – have taken pride in the notion that this was the first Masonic lodge in Scotland, a fact that is the cause of no little argument among those who are happy to describe themselves, as Burns was, as members of the fellowship. The Mother Lodge is tucked under the tower of the old abbey, about halfway down the now pedestrianised

Main Street. I grew up in Kilwinning. I used to walk past this elegant building as a boy, and I always wondered what it was for. I was really much more intrigued than frightened, and for all it looked out of bounds, I hoped that I might one day get inside, the way I hoped they'd eventually let me into all the buildings that were meant for adults. The committee had asked me to come and give the 'Address to Kilwinning' at their Bicentennial Burns Supper. I booked the train right away, and put on my long trousers.

People who go to social clubs are always punctual. They formed a line outside, waiting for the doors to open. The members of the committee, and those due to speak, first went to the men-only bar downstairs. There were whiskies going round at speed, and I got into conversation with a jolly guy who liked the idea that I'd recently been to some of the snowed-over farms in south Ayrshire. He started telling me that he'd done farmwork from the age of twelve or thirteen, how hard it was, how badly paid. The man with the bagpipes was prac-tising in the club's museum. We got into a line ourselves before long – according to where we'd be sitting at the top table – and off we went, the piper at the front, up the stairs and into a room full of clapping people. I felt I needed a drink, but before I could feel it again every tumbler on the table was full. My mother sat across the room; she looked nice, having a good time with her friends. She waved over conspiratorially. I had a feeling she'd somehow got me into this.

Just about everybody there spoke in the accent Burns would have spoken in. The poetry just tripped out of them, the songs turned over in their mouths like soft potatoes. The president cheered them along with his comical words. All the struggles and arguments and worries to do with Burns were not to be noticed here; this was a celebration of wit and sentiment, of sociability, and the humour of the poems never felt more familiar. The lines of 'Holy Willie's Prayer' and 'Tam o' Shanter' were performed by a man with one of those very Burnsian faces, very Burnsian tongues, and extremely Burnsian names – Bill Dunlop.

All around the room, faces were rocking to the songs of Robert Burns. This was the 200th anniversary. There was clapping and a clattering of dishes, a clinking of glasses and raising of toasts; a haggis was addressed and split and served; whisky was drunk; and the strip-lights burned like beacons. There are many Robert Burnses, many of them, and none of them the same. There are as many Robert Burnses as there are people to care for him, and things to care for. As his funeral cortège made its slow way down the main street in Dumfries, a little boy was heard to say to his mother, 'But who will be our poet now?' The answer, after all this time, is: 'He will.' The glass in front of me was full again, and the lights had settled down. It was time for me to speak. Time to toast this town of mine, and the complicated memory of Robert Burns.

This volume grew out of a spirit of sociability: we wanted to fashion a book of Burns's best poems that would also include a story of how he might be read today. I thought it likely that Burns would object to the idea that the fun should be taken out of literature, and I wanted to restore it, at least in this edition, by sorting the work so as to greet that argument. Canonical writers are not always best served by their canonisers: the threat of the 'set text' is very great, and we must allow ourselves to light on ways to ensure that a solemn presentation of greatness in a writer does not, for all its scholarly virtues, result in the writer remaining unread.

The poems I've chosen have found their way into four overarching categories: the lasses, the drinks, the immortals and the politics. Of course, the categories bleed into one another, but if you allow that this arrangement causes the poems to suggest one another in new ways, then you might forgive the insult my arrangement offers to chronology. There are great poems left out and, some would say, dubious ones left in, but I wanted to bring readers with me on a personal journey and a confrontation with the glory of the poet's work. It is for me the summation of many journeys, and this night out with Robert Burns confirms my feeling that he is the prince of poetry, not only for me or for Scotland, but for the world. It might have pleased the long-dead boy beside the funeral cortège to know that Burns is indeed our poet — now, and for as long as the world has a care and a feeling for the dance of reality and imagination.

The Lasses

In the best work of the world's most representative poet, every word can sound like an effusion of pure spirit. And who could mistake Burns's genius when they encounter his beautiful lyric 'Green Grow the Rashes'? He once introduced it by saying the song was written in 'the genuine language of my heart'. A hymn to spontaneous affection over worldly desires, there is nothing else like it. I once knew a retired Ayrshire sailor, Mr Savage. I remember him singing this song one morning as he made his way along the seafront in the town of Saltcoats. The Firth of Clyde appeared to calm itself at the sound of the old man's voice, as he sang this lilting memorial to a great and simple sentiment.

Green Grow the Rashes

Green grow the rashes, O;
Green grow the rashes, O;
The sweetest hours that e'er I spend,
  Are spent amang the lasses, O.

There's nought but care on ev'ry han',
  In ev'ry hour that passes, O:
What signifies the life o' man,
  An' 'twere na for the lasses, O.
        Green grow, &c.

The warly race may riches chase,
  An' riches still may fly them, O;
An' tho' at last they catch them fast,
  Their hearts can ne'er enjoy them, O.
        Green grow, &c.

But gie me a canny hour at e'en,
  My arms about my Dearie, O;
An' warly cares, an' warly men,
  May a' gae tapsalteerie, O!
        Green grow, &c.

For you sae douse, ye sneer at this,
  Ye're nought but senseless asses, O:
The wisest Man the warl' saw,
  He dearly lov'd the lasses, O.
        Green grow, &c.

Auld Nature swears, the lovely Dears
  Her noblest work she classes, O:
Her prentice han' she try'd on man,
  An' then she made the lasses, O.
        Green grow, &c.

One can practically see the yellow light at the window of the dance-hall and feel the pulse of romantic hope, a new and lively element in the blood. And here she is, Mary Morison – as 'the dance gaed through the lighted ha'' – and we are caught immediately in the drama of her specialness. There is a grave in Mauchline churchyard to 'the poet's bonnie Mary Morison, who died on 29 June 1791, aged 20'. Mary is a ghost among the drinking glasses, yet forever alive in the flow of these images.

Mary Morison

O Mary, at thy window be,
　It is the wish'd, the trysted hour;
Those smiles and glances let me see,
　That make the miser's treasure poor:
How blythely wad I bide the stoure,
　A weary slave frae sun to sun;
Could I the rich reward secure,
　The lovely Mary Morison!

Yestreen when to the trembling string
　The dance gaed through the lighted ha',
To thee my fancy took its wing,
　I sat, but neither heard, nor saw:
Though this was fair, and that was braw,
　And yon the toast of a' the town,
I sigh'd, and said amang them a',
　'Ye are na Mary Morison.'

O Mary, canst thou wreck his peace,
　Wha for thy sake wad gladly die!
Or canst thou break that heart of his,
　Whase only faute is loving thee!
If love for love thou wilt na gie,
　At least be pity to me shown;
A thought ungentle canna be
　The thought o' Mary Morison.

I wrote part of my first novel, *Our Fathers*, in the west of Ireland, alone in a house by the sea in County Cork. After dark, a regular beam of light from the Fastnet lighthouse would fall over the bed and I woke there one night with a weathered thought. It was to do with the Irish who had left for Scotland years before. I went back to my desk and wrote some lines about the main character's father, Tam. He 'once wrote a letter to a cousin in Ireland, saying that he only stuck to the farm because of Robert Burns. "My habits are bad in the field," he wrote, "but never mind, there's something to see in the battle for stuff over here, with the thought of the poet's hand there beside you."' Tam then goes to the Ayrshire madhouse at Glengall and sings 'The Belles of Mauchline' to his sick wife, and he kisses her.

The Belles of Mauchline

In Mauchline there dwells six proper young Belles,
  The pride of the place and its neighbourhood a',
Their carriage and dress a stranger would guess,
  In Lon'on or Paris they'd gotten it a':
Miss Miller is fine, Miss Murkland's divine,
  Miss Smith she has wit and Miss Betty is braw;
There's beauty and fortune to get wi' Miss Morton,
  But ARMOUR's the jewel for me o' them a'.—

Burns had intended to emigrate with Mary Campbell to Jamaica, but she died in Greenock before they could leave. Each of Burns's lasses has a skirl of the country dance-hall about her and a scent of the Ayrshire fields, but not Mary. We imagine her spirit mingled with high foreign hopes and sea salt, caught up in the Atlantic roar.

Will Ye Go to the Indies, My Mary?

Will ye go to the Indies, my Mary,
  And leave auld Scotia's shore;
Will ye go to the Indies, my Mary,
  Across th' Atlantic roar.

O sweet grows the lime and the orange
  And the apple on the pine;
But a' the charms o' the Indies
  Can never equal thine.

I hae sworn by the Heavens to my Mary,
  I hae sworn by the Heavens to be true;
And sae may the Heavens forget me,
  When I forget my vow!

O plight me your faith, my Mary,
  And plight me your lily-white hand;
O plight me your faith, my Mary,
  Before I leave Scotia's strand.

We hae plighted our truth, my Mary,
  In mutual affection to join:
And curst be the cause that shall part us,
  The hour, and the moment o' time!!!

A love poem is a sudden encounter with one's own capacity for wonder; it is a settlement of joy amid the complications of affection. 'A lyric poem,' writes James Fenton, 'expresses an intense feeling of the moment. It is all about the subjective, all about the here and now. It is not – alas, for the loved one – a contract, or a prenuptial agreement.'

Of A' the Airts

Of a' the airts the wind can blaw,
  I dearly like the West;
For there the bony Lassie lives,
  The Lassie I lo'e best:
There's wild-woods grow, and rivers row,
  And mony a hill between;
But day and night my fancy's flight
  Is ever wi' my Jean.—

I see her in the dewy flowers,
  I see her sweet and fair;
I hear her in the tunefu' birds,
  I hear her charm the air:
There's not a bony flower, that springs
  By fountain, shaw, or green;
There's not a bony bird that sings
  But minds me o' my Jean.—

I once sang this song in a gymnasium filled to the summit of the wall bars with tittering Ayrshire schoolchildren. It was St Luke's Primary School in the spring of 1978, and Mrs Ferguson, the headmistress, had decided there was only one boy for the job. I can still see my blushing face beside the old piano, and Fergie's vaguely nationalistic smile as she thumped the keys and nodded me in with a skoosh of pride. It wasn't entirely easy – aged ten – to conjure up my troubles with the saucy lasses, but from the corner of my eye I saw the girls coming into the gym ready for Jacqueline Thompson's ballet class, due to begin as soon as the Burns was over. The lasses were all hair-buns and slipperettes, and I know my voice lifted and reached out to meet the loveliness of their wicked faces.

My Love She's but a Lassie Yet

My love she's but a lassie yet,
My love she's but a lassie yet;
We'll let her stand a year or twa,
   She'll no be half sae saucy yet.——

I rue the day I sought her O,
I rue the day I sought her O,
Wha gets her needs na say he's woo'd,
   But he may say he's bought her O.——

Come draw a drap o' the best o't yet,
Come draw a drap o' the best o't yet:
Gae seek for Pleasure whare ye will,
   But here I never misst it yet.——

We're a' dry wi' drinkin o't,
We're a' dry wi' drinkin o't:
The minister kisst the fidler's wife,
   He could na preach for thinkin o't.——

Robert Burns saw love as an expression of natural freedom, but he understood well enough that it might also be experienced as a mode of performance. In Edinburgh, he fell for a married lady, Agnes McLehose, or Nancy, who lived alone in Potter Row, and he turned their brief affair into a sometimes rapturous drama of drawing-room manners. They took arcadian names, Clarinda and Sylvander, and played their respective parts in a way that offered no great insult to sincerity. 'Ae Fond Kiss' is proof of that: the final stanza, said Walter Scott, 'contains the essence of a thousand love tales'.

Ae Fond Kiss

Ae fond kiss, and then we sever;
Ae fareweel, and then for ever!
Deep in heart-wrung tears I'll pledge thee,
Warring sighs and groans I'll wage thee.——

Who shall say that Fortune grieves him,
While the star of hope she leaves him:
Me, nae chearful twinkle lights me;
Dark despair around benights me.——

I'll ne'er blame my partial fancy,
Naething could resist my Nancy:
But to see her, was to love her;
Love but her, and love for ever.——

Had we never lov'd sae kindly,
Had we never lov'd sae blindly!
Never met—or never parted,
We had ne'er been broken-hearted.——

Fare-thee-weel, thou first and fairest!
Fare-thee-weel, thou best and dearest!
Thine be ilka joy and treasure,
Peace, Enjoyment, Love and Pleasure!——

Ae fond kiss, and then we sever!
Ae fareweel, Alas, for ever!
Deep in heart-wrung tears I'll pledge thee,
Warring sighs and groans I'll wage thee.—

A *birk* is a silver birch tree. It has a talent for growing in poor soil and a lifespan between sixty and ninety years. The bark is usually white and smooth, the twigs are waxy, and fresh green foliage appears to dress the trees in spring. The unobtrusive flowers appear in April and the small fruits in June.

Afton Water

Flow gently, sweet Afton, among thy green braes,
Flow gently, I'll sing thee a song in thy praise;
My Mary's asleep by thy murmuring stream,
Flow gently, sweet Afton, disturb not her dream.

Thou stock dove whose echo resounds thro' the glen,
Ye wild whistling blackbirds in yon thorny den,
Thou green crested lapwing thy screaming forbear,
I charge you disturb not my slumbering Fair.

How lofty, sweet Afton, thy neighbouring hills,
Far mark'd with the courses of clear, winding rills;
There daily I wander as noon rises high,
My flocks and my Mary's sweet Cot in my eye.

How pleasant thy banks and green vallies below,
Where wild in the woodlands the primroses blow;
There oft as mild ev'ning weeps over the lea,
The sweet scented birk shades my Mary and me.

Thy chrystal stream, Afton, how lovely it glides,
And winds by the cot where my Mary resides;
How wanton thy waters her snowy feet lave,
As gathering sweet flowerets she stems thy clear wave.

Flow gently, sweet Afton, among thy green braes,
Flow gently, sweet River, the theme of my lays;
My Mary's asleep by thy murmuring stream,
Flow gently, sweet Afton, disturb not her dream.

enneth McKellar sings it with the sonority of the truly smitten. Peter Morrison sings it more expansively, as if he were gathering the earth's purest elements into a single song. Jean Redpath sings it as if she were reaching gently for the impossible and Ed Miller sings it wistfully, as if he were addressing a girl from a passing train. Eddi Reader brings to it a beautiful native airiness and Robert Wilson packs it with regret. Peter McCutcheon sings it as if through a fog of self-involvement and Carly Simon as if she were California dreaming. Davy Steele brings it home, investing the words with a simple belief and a show of love. But though Burns had many lasses, for me there can only be one – Mrs McGrath, a traditional Scottish singer, whose un-accompanied version is a wonderful feat of intimacy. She sings as if she intended the song for oneself alone.

A Red Red Rose

O my Luve's like a red, red rose,
  That's newly sprung in June;
O my Luve's like the melodie
  That's sweetly play'd in tune.——

As fair art thou, my bonie lass,
  So deep in luve am I;
And I will love thee still, my Dear,
  Till a' the seas gang dry.——

Till a' the seas gang dry, my Dear,
  And the rocks melt wi' the sun:
I will love thee still, my Dear,
  While the sands o' life shall run.——

And fare thee weel, my only Luve!
  And fare thee weel, a while!
And I will come again, my Luve,
  Tho' it were ten thousand mile!

As Burns lay dying at his house, the Mill Vennel at Dumfries, a girl who lived across the road would come each day to comfort him and assist his wife. Her name was Jessy Lewars and she played the harpsichord, causing Burns to ponder her sweetness and imagine himself in love with her.

Oh Wert Thou in the Cauld Blast

Oh wert thou in the cauld blast,
  On yonder lea, on yonder lea;
My plaidie to the angry airt,
  I'd shelter thee, I'd shelter thee:
Or did misfortune's bitter storms
  Around thee blaw, around thee blaw,
Thy bield should be my bosom,
  To share it a', to share it a'.

Or were I in the wildest waste,
  Sae black and bare, sae black and bare,
The desart were a paradise,
  If thou wert there, if thou wert there.
Or were I monarch o' the globe,
  Wi' thee to reign, wi' thee to reign;
The brightest jewel in my crown,
  Wad be my queen, wad be my queen.

The summer is gone and the lasses with it, but Burns was minded to dwell on the beauty and promise of the young. He is to me the poet of human growth. And here we have it: the pride felt by Mary Ann at the sight of her laddie is also a mark of trust in the power of regeneration. Leaves may fall, but only to compost the wide earth, and better days lie ahead. At Eglinton Park in Kilwinning I once found these words written on a sheet of paper and stuffed between a crack in the rocks.

Lady Mary Ann

O Lady Mary Ann looks o'er the castle-wa',
She saw three bonie boys playing at the ba',
The youngest he was the flower amang them a',
My bonie laddie's young but he's growin yet.—

O Father, O Father, an ye think it fit,
We'll send him a year to the College yet,
We'll sew a green ribban round about his hat,
And that will let them ken he's to marry yet.—

Lady Mary Ann was a flower in the dew,
Sweet was its smell and bonie was its hue,
And the langer it blossom'd, the sweeter it grew,
For the lily in the bud will be bonier yet.—

Young Charlie Cochran was the sprout of an aik,
Bonie, and bloomin and straught was its make,
The sun took delight to shine for its sake,
And it will be the brag o' the forest yet.—

The Simmer is gane when the leaves they were green,
And the days are awa that we hae seen,
But far better days I trust will come again,
For my bonie laddie's young but he's growin yet.—

B urns had thirteen children and was able to cast the best of what he felt for their mothers – those lively sweetheart lasses – as beneficent light on the little ones, in every case honouring the joy of their conception. With the servant-girl Betsy Paton he had his first daughter, Betty, whom he welcomes into her role as the apple of her father's eye.

A Poet's Welcome to His Love-Begotten Daughter; the First Instance that Entitled Him to the Venerable Appellation of Father

Thou's welcome, Wean! Mischanter fa' me,
If thoughts o' thee, or yet thy Mamie,
Shall ever daunton me or awe me,
      My bonie lady;
Or if I blush when thou shalt ca' me
      Tyta, or Daddie.—

Tho' now they ca' me, Fornicator,
And tease my name in kintra clatter,
The mair they talk, I'm kend the better;
      E'en let them clash!
An auld wife's tongue's a feckless matter
      To gie ane fash.—

Welcome! My bonie, sweet, wee Dochter!
Tho' ye come here a wee unsought for;
And tho' your comin I hae fought for,
      Baith Kirk and Queir;
Yet by my faith, ye're no unwrought for,
      That I shall swear!

Wee image o' my bonie Betty,
As fatherly I kiss and daut thee,
As dear and near my heart I set thee,
   Wi' as gude will,
As a' the Priests had seen me get thee
   That's out o' hell.——

Sweet fruit o' monie a merry dint,
My funny toil is no a' tint;
Tho' ye come to the warld asklent,
   Which fools may scoff at,
In my last plack thy part's be in't,
   The better half o't.——

Tho' I should be the waur bestead,
Thou's be as braw and bienly clad,
And thy young years as nicely bred
   Wi' education,
As ony brat o' Wedlock's bed,
   In a' thy station.——

Lord grant that thou may ay inherit
Thy Mither's looks an' gracefu' merit;
An' thy poor, worthless Daddie's spirit,
   Without his failins!
'Twad please me mair to see thee heir it
   Than stocked mailins!

For if thou be, what I wad hae thee,
And tak the counsel I shall gie thee,
I'll never rue my trouble wi' thee,
   The cost nor shame o't,
But be a loving Father to thee,
   And brag the name o't.——

My daughter was born in a room of smiles that stands above the London traffic. And late that night, as her mother slept and the ward stood quiet with its vases of flowers, I carried Nell to a room of cots and washed her in a bath of warm water. The miracle was her face and the sound of the ticking clock: could we hear the trees that shushed in Regent's Park at that ungodly hour? My daughter smiled and looked straight up as her father stumbled to promise her heaven and earth. In that dark room, I tilted our baby in the water tray as if she were a developing print of an old photograph. Her vital toes pawed the air. At last every inch of her was clear to me and I kissed her as I wrapped her in a towel, reciting the words of Robert Burns's first poem.

Handsome Nell

O once I lov'd a bonnie lass,
  An' aye I love her still,
An' whilst that virtue warms my breast
  I'll love my handsome Nell.

As bonnie lasses I hae seen,
  And mony full as braw,
But for a modest gracefu' mein
  The like I never saw.

A bonny lass I will confess,
  Is pleasant to the e'e,
But without some better qualities
  She's no a lass for me.

But Nelly's looks are blythe and sweet,
  And what is best of a',
Her reputation is compleat,
  And fair without a flaw;

She dresses ay sae clean and neat,
  Both decent and genteel;
And then there's something in her gait
  Gars ony dress look weel.

A gaudy dress and gentle air
  May slightly touch the heart,
But it's innocence and modesty
  That polishes the dart.

'Tis this in Nelly pleases me,
  'Tis this enchants my soul;
For absolutely in my breast
  She reigns without control.

The Drinks

Whisky Collins

large Scotch whisky
two clicks of lemon juice
dash of sugar syrup
soda water (chilled)
slice of lemon

Shake up the Scotch, lemon juice and sugar syrup in a shaker. Pour into a tall glass and top up with soda. Add a slice of lemon.

Scotch Drink

Gie him strong Drink *until he wink,*
  That's sinking in despair;
An' liquor *guid, to fire his bluid,*
  That's prest wi' grief an' care:
There let him bowse an' deep carouse,
  Wi' bumpers flowing o'er,
Till he forgets his loves *or debts,*
  An' minds his griefs no more.
                    Solomon's Proverbs, xxxi:6, 7

Let other Poets raise a fracas
'Bout vines, an' wines, an' druken *Bacchus,*
An' crabbed names an' stories wrack us,
            An' grate our lug,
I sing the juice *Scotch bear* can mak us,
            In glass or jug.

O thou, my MUSE! Guid, auld SCOTCH DRINK!
Whether thro' wimplin worms thou jink,
Or, richly brown, ream owre the brink,
            In glorious faem,
Inspire me, till I lisp an' *wink,*
            To sing thy name!

Let husky Wheat the haughs adorn,
And Aits set up their awnie horn,
An' Pease an' Beans, at een or morn,
                Perfume the plain,
Leeze me on thee *John Barleycorn*,
                Thou king o' grain!

On thee aft Scotland chows her cood,
In souple scones, the wale o' food!
Or tumbling in the boiling flood
                Wi' kail an' beef;
But when thou pours thy strong *heart's blood*,
                There thou shines chief.

Food fills the wame, an' keeps us livin:
Tho' life's a gift no worth receivin,
When heavy-dragg'd wi' pine an' grievin;
                But oil'd by thee,
The wheels o' life gae down-hill, scrievin,
                Wi' rattlin glee.

Thou clears the head o' doited Lear;
Thou chears the heart o' drooping Care;
Thou strings the nerves o' Labor-sair,
                At's weary toil;
Thou ev'n brightens dark Despair,
                Wi' gloomy smile.

Aft, clad in massy, siller weed,
Wi' Gentles thou erects thy head;
Yet, humbly kind, in time o' need,
        The *poorman*'s wine,
His wee drap pirratch, or his bread,
        Thou kitchens fine.

Thou art the life o' public haunts;
But thee, what were our fairs an' rants?
Ev'n goodly meetings o' the saunts,
        By thee inspir'd,
When gaping they besiege the *tents*,
        Are doubly fir'd.

That *merry night* we get the corn in
O sweetly, then, thou reams the horn in!
Or reekan on a *New-year-mornin*
        In cog or bicker,
An' just a wee drap *sp'ritual burn* in,
        An' *gusty sucker*!

When Vulcan gies his bellys breath,
An' Ploughmen gather wi' their graith,
O rare! to see thee fizz an' fraeth
        I' the lugget caup!
Then *Burnewin* comes on like Death,
        At ev'ry chap.

Nae mercy, then, for airn *or* steel;
The brawnie, banie, Ploughman-chiel
Brings hard owrehip, wi' sturdy wheel,
            The strong forehammer,
Till block an' studdie ring an' reel
            Wi' dinsome clamour.

When skirlin weanies see the light,
Though maks the gossips clatter bright,
How fumbling coofs their dearies slight,
            Wae worth the name!
Nae Howdie gets a social night,
            Or plack frae them.

When neebors anger at a plea,
An' just as wud as wud can be,
How easy can the *barley-bree*
            Cement the quarrel!
It's ay the cheapest Lawyer's fee
            To taste the barrel.

Alake! that e'er my *Muse* has reason
To wyte her countrymen wi' treason!
But mony daily weet their weason
            Wi' liquors nice,
An' hardly, in a winter season,
            E'er spier her price.

Wae worth that *Brandy*, burnan trash!
Fell source o' monie a pain an' brash!
Twins mony a poor, doylt, druken hash
        O' half his days;
An' sends, beside, auld *Scotland*'s cash
        To her warst faes.

Ye Scots wha wish auld Scotland well,
Ye chief, to you my tale I tell,
Poor, plackless devils like *mysel*,
        It sets you ill,
Wi' bitter, dearthfu' *wines* to mell,
        Or *foreign gill*.

May *Gravels* round his blather wrench,
An' *Gouts* torment him, inch by inch,
Wha twists his gruntle wi' a glunch
        O' sour disdain,
Out owre a glass o' *Whisky-punch*
        Wi' honest men!

O *Whisky*! soul o' plays an' pranks!
Accept a *Bardie*'s gratefu' thanks!
When wanting thee, what tuneless cranks
        Are my poor Verses!
Thou comes—they rattle i' their ranks
        At ither's arses!

Thee, *Ferintosh*! O sadly lost!
Scotland lament frae coast to coast!
Now colic-grips, an' barkin hoast,
      May kill us a';
For loyal *Forbes' Charter'd boast*
      Is taen awa!

Thae curst horse-leeches o' th' Excise,
Wha mak the *Whisky stills* their prize!
Haud up thy han' *Deil*! ance, twice, thrice!
      There, seize the blinkers!
An' bake them up in brunstane pies
      For poor damn'd *Drinkers*.

Fortune, if thou'll but gie me still
Hale breeks, a scone, an' *Whisky gill*,
An' rowth o' *rhyme* to rave at will,
      Tak a' the rest,
An' deal't about as thy blind skill
      Directs thee best.

S ean O'Casey's *The Silver Tassie* was rejected by the Abbey Theatre in 1928, mainly on account of W.B. Yeats's certainty that the play had no real subject. But it has always lived in my mind, as much as anything for its echo of Burns's song. Harry Heegan is on leave from the Great War and back among his own people. They are celebrating a sporting victory and the cup that came with it, when Harry turns to Barney, his friend from the Front.

HARRY: The song that the little Jock used to sing, Barney, what was it? The little Jock we left shrivellin' on the wire after the last push?

BARNEY: 'Will Ye No Come Back Again?'

HARRY: No, no, the one we all used to sing with him, 'The Silver Tassie'. [*pointing to cup*] There it is, the Silver Tassie, won by the odd goal in five kicked by Harry Heegan.

After a moment the drink breaks out and they pin their energies to a lust for drams. It is a scene and a half: that song left dangling with the little Jock on the wire, and the silver cup filled with drink as if it were the very medicine for us all.

BARNEY [*taking a bottle of wine from his pocket*]: Empty her of her virtues, eh?

HARRY: Spill it out, Barney, spill it out . . . [*seizing silver cup, and holding it towards Barney*] Here, into the cup, be-God. A drink out of the cup, out of the Silver Tassie!

BARNEY [*who has removed the cap and taken out the cork*]: Here she is now . . . Ready for anything, stripp'd to the skin!

The Silver Tassie

Go fetch to me a pint o' wine,
  And fill it in a silver tassie;
That I may drink, before I go,
  A service to my bonie lassie:
The boat rocks at the Pier o' Leith,
  Fu' loud the wind blaws frae the Ferry,
The ship rides by the Berwick-law,
  And I maun leave my bony Mary.

The trumpets sound, the banners fly,
  The glittering spears are ranked ready,
The shouts o' war are heard afar,
  The battle closes deep and bloody.
It's not the roar o' sea or shore,
  Wad make me langer wish to tarry;
Nor shouts o' war that's heard afar—
  It's leaving thee, my bony Mary!

One recent April – daffodils waving by the roadside – I took Seamus Heaney and Karl Miller for a drive through the land of Robert Burns. Seamus later called the trip miraculous: the wild Ayrshire rains and the Doon water, with jokes exchanged and histories kindled. Seamus stood apart at one point in the slanted graveyard at Kirk Alloway, consorting with Latin phrases on the headstone to Burns's father, and I'm sure Karl and I were thinking the same thought, about Seamus's own father and the image of him inscribed years ago in the poem 'Digging'. It is a poem that brings Seamus into company with Robert Burns, and such thoughts had made us laugh a minute before when we passed the Tam o' Shanter Experience.

'Soon,' said Karl with an evil grin, 'it'll be the Seamus Heaney Experience.'

'That's right,' said Seamus. 'A few churns and a confessional box.'

Up on Alloway Brig, where Tam's grey mare, Meg, loses her tail and gains a legend, we stood and smiled to be at the centre of the imagined life of that great poem. Never for me has the written word and the stony ground existed in such an easy state of brotherhood, and as the rain came on we went off to drink a whisky more flavoured than reality.

Tam o' Shanter — A Tale

Of Brownyis and of Bogillis full is this buke.

Gawin Douglas

When chapman billies leave the street,
And drouthy neebors, neebors meet,
As market-days are wearing late,
An' folk begin to tak the gate;
While we sit bousing at the nappy,
And getting fou and unco happy,
We think na on the lang Scots miles,
The mosses, waters, slaps, and styles,
That lie between us and our hame,
Whare sits our sulky sullen dame,
Gathering her brows like gathering storm,
Nursing her wrath to keep it warm.

This truth fand honest *Tam o' Shanter*,
As he frae Ayr ae night did canter,
(Auld Ayr, wham ne'er a town surpasses,
For honest men and bonny lasses.)

O *Tam*! hadst thou but been sae wise,
As ta'en thy ain wife *Kate*'s advice!
She tauld thee weel thou was a skellum,
A blethering, blustering, drunken blellum;
That frae November till October,
Ae market-day thou was nae sober;
That ilka melder, wi' the miller,
Thou sat as lang as thou had siller;

That every naig was ca'd a shoe on,
The smith and thee gat roaring fou on;
That at the Lord's house, even on Sunday,
Thou drank wi' Kirkton Jean till Monday.
She prophesied that late or soon,
Thou would be found deep drown'd in Doon;
Or catch'd wi' warlocks in the mirk,
By *Alloway*'s auld haunted kirk.

Ah, gentle dames! it gars me greet,
To think how mony counsels sweet,
How mony lengthen'd sage advices,
The husband frae the wife despises!

But to our tale: Ae market-night,
Tam had got planted unco right;
Fast by an ingle, bleezing finely,
Wi' reaming swats, that drank divinely;
And at his elbow, Souter *Johnny*,
His ancient, trusty, drouthy crony;
Tam lo'ed him like a vera brither;
They had been fou for weeks thegither.
The night drave on wi' sangs and clatter;
And ay the ale was growing better:
The landlady and *Tam* grew gracious,
Wi' favours, secret, sweet, and precious:
The Souter tauld his queerest stories;
The landlord's laugh was ready chorus:
The storm without might rair and rustle,
Tam did na mind the storm a whistle.

Care, mad to see a man sae happy,
E'en drown'd himsel amang the nappy:
As bees flee hame wi' lades o' treasure,
The minutes wing'd their way wi' pleasure:
Kings may be blest, but *Tam* was glorious,
O'er a' the ills o' life victorious!

But pleasures are like poppies spread,
You seize the flower, its bloom is shed;
Or like the snow falls in the river,
A moment white—then melts for ever;
Or like the borealis race,
That flit ere you can point their place;
Or like the rainbow's lovely form
Evanishing amid the storm.—
Nae man can tether time or tide;
The hour approaches *Tam* maun ride;
That hour, o' night's black arch the key-stane,
That dreary hour he mounts his beast in;
And sic a night he taks the road in,
As ne'er poor sinner was abroad in.

The wind blew as 'twad blawn its last;
The rattling showers rose on the blast;
The speedy gleams the darkness swallow'd;
Loud, deep, and lang, the thunder bellow'd:
That night, a child might understand,
The Deil had business on his hand.

Weel mounted on his gray mare, *Meg*,
A better never lifted leg,
Tam skelpit on thro' dub and mire,
Despising wind, and rain, and fire;
Whiles holding fast his gude blue bonnet;
Whiles crooning o'er some auld Scots sonnet;
Whiles glowring round wi' prudent cares,
Lest bogles catch him unawares:
Kirk-Alloway was drawing nigh,
Whare ghaists and houlets nightly cry.—

By this time he was cross the ford,
Whare, in the snaw, the chapman smoor'd;
And past the birks and meikle stane,
Where drunken *Charlie* brak's neck-bane;
And thro' the whins, and by the cairn,
Where hunters fand the murder'd bairn;
And near the thorn, aboon the well,
Where *Mungo*'s mither hang'd hersel.—
Before him *Doon* pours all his floods;
The doubling storm roars thro' the woods;
The lightnings flash from pole to pole;
Near and more near the thunders roll:
When, glimmering thro' the groaning trees,
Kirk-Alloway seem'd in a bleeze;
Thro' ilka bore the beams were glancing;
And loud resounded mirth and dancing.—

Inspiring bold *John Barleycorn*!
What dangers thou canst make us scorn!
Wi' tippeny, we fear nae evil;
Wi' usquabae, we'll face the devil!——
The swats sae ream'd in *Tammie*'s noddle,
Fair play, he car'd na deils a boddle.
But *Maggie* stood right sair astonish'd,
Till, by the heel and hand admonish'd,
She ventured forward on the light;
And, vow! *Tam* saw an unco sight!
Warlocks and witches in a dance;
Nae cotillion brent new frae *France*,
But hornpipes, jigs, strathspeys, and reels,
Put life and mettle in their heels.
A winnock-bunker in the east,
There sat auld Nick, in shape o' beast;
A towzie tyke, black, grim, and large,
To gie them music was his charge:
He screw'd the pipes and gart them skirl,
Till roof and rafters a' did dirl.——
Coffins stood round, like open presses,
That shaw'd the dead in their last dresses;
And by some devilish cantraip slight
Each in its cauld hand held a light.——
By which heroic *Tam* was able
To note upon the haly table,
A murderer's banes, in gibbet airns;
Twa span-lang, wee, unchristen'd bairns;
A thief, new-cutted frae a rape,
Wi' his last gasp his gab did gape;
Five tomahawks, wi' blude red-rusted;
Five scymitars, wi' murder crusted;
A garter, which a babe had strangled;
A knife, a father's throat had mangled,

Whom his ain son o' life bereft,
The grey hairs yet stack to the heft;
Three Lawyers' tongues, turn'd inside out,
Wi' lies seam'd like a beggar's clout;
Three Priests' hearts, rotten, black as muck,
Lay stinking, vile, in every neuk.——

As *Tammie* glowr'd, amaz'd, and curious,
The mirth and fun grew fast and furious:
The piper loud and louder blew;
The dancers quick and quicker flew;
The reel'd, they set, they cross'd, they cleekit,
Till ilka carlin swat and reekit,
And coost her duddies to the wark,
And linket at it in her sark!

Now *Tam*, O *Tam*! had thae been queans,
A' plump and strapping in their teens,
Their sarks, instead o' creeshie flannen,
Been snaw-white seventeen hunder linnen!
Thir breeks o' mine, my only pair,
That ance were plush, o' gude blue hair,
I wad hae gi'en them off my hurdies,
For ae blink o' the bonie burdies!

But wither'd beldams, auld and droll,
Rigwoodie hags wad spean a foal,
Lowping and flinging on a crummock.
I wonder didna turn thy stomach.

But *Tam* kend what was what fu' brawlie,
There was ae winsome wench and wawlie,
That night enlisted in the core,
(Lang after kend on *Carrick* shore;
For mony a beast to dead she shot,
And perish'd mony a bony boat,
And shook baith meikle corn and bear,
And kept the country-side in fear:)
Her cutty sark, o' Paisley harn,
That while a lassie she had worn,
In longitude tho' sorely scanty,
It was her best, and she was vauntic.—
Ah! little kend thy reverend grannie,
That sark she coft for her wee Nannie,
Wi' twa pund Scots, ('twas a' her riches),
Wad ever grac'd a dance of witches!

But here my Muse her wing maun cour;
Sic flights are far beyond her pow'r;
To sing how Nannie lap and flang,
(A souple jade she was, and strang),
And how *Tam* stood, like ane bewitch'd,
And thought his very een enrich'd;
Even Satan glowr'd, and fidg'd fu' fain,
And hotch'd and blew wi' might and main:
Till first ae caper, syne anither,
Tam tint his reason a' thegither,
And roars out, 'Weel done, Cutty-sark!'
And in an instant all was dark:
And scarcely had he Maggie rallied,
When out the hellish legion sallied.

As bees bizz out wi' angry fyke,
When plundering herds assail their byke;
As open pussie's mortal foes,
When, pop! she starts before their nose;
As eager runs the market-crowd,
When 'Catch the thief!' resounds aloud;
So Maggie runs, the witches follow,
Wi' mony an eldritch skreech and hollow.

Ah, *Tam*! Ah, *Tam*! thou'll get thy fairin!
In hell, they'll roast thee like a herrin!
In vain thy *Kate* awaits thy comin!
Kate soon will be a woefu' woman!
Now, do thy speedy utmost, Meg,
And win the key-stane[1] of the brig;
There at them thou thy tail may toss,
A running stream they dare na cross.
But ere the key-stane she could make,
The fient a tail she had to shake!
For Nannie, far before the rest,
Hard upon noble Maggie prest,
And flew at *Tam* wi' furious ettle;
But little wist she Maggie's mettle—
Ae spring brought off her master hale,
But left behind her ain gray tail:
The carlin claught her by the rump,
And left poor Maggie scarce a stump.

[1] It is a well known fact that witches, or any evil spirits, have no power to follow a poor wight any farther than the middle of the next running stream.—It may be proper likewise to mention to the benighted traveller, that when he falls in with *bogles*, whatever danger may be in his going forward, there is much more hazard in turning back.

Now, wha this tale o' truth shall read,
Ilk man and mother's son, take heed:
Whene'er to drink you are inclin'd,
Or cutty-sarks run in your mind,
Think, ye may buy the joys o'er dear,
Remember Tam o' Shanter's mare.

'Auld Scotland has a raucle tongue,' writes Burns, well-oiled, if chance should favour, with words and whisky. More than any other poet, Burns saw liberty and whisky going together; he would study politics 'over a glass of guid auld *Scotch Drink*' in the bothy at Nance Tinnock's in Mauchline, and nothing could raise his hackles like the threat of English tax on the aqua vitae. You get the feeling that Burns's nights at the pub were hot with irony: for him the frisky juice can make a man see straight, while others squint as they thirst for power.

The Author's Earnest Cry and Prayer, to the Right Honorable and Honorable, the Scotch Representatives in the House of Commons[1]

Dearest of Distillation! last and best!——
——How art thou lost!——

Parody on Milton

Ye Irish lords, ye *knights* an' *squires*,
Wha represent our BRUGHS an' SHIRES,
An' dousely manage our affairs
      In *Parliament*,
To you a simple Bardie's pray'rs
      Are humbly sent.

Alas! my roupet *Muse* is haerse!
Your Honors' hearts wi' grief 'twad pierce,
To see her sittan on her arse
      Low i' the dust,
An' scriechan out prosaic verse,
      An' like to brust!

[1] This was wrote before the Act anent the Scotch Distilleries, of session 1786; for which Scotland and the Author return their most grateful thanks.

Tell them wha hae the chief direction,
Scotland and *me*'s in great affliction,
E'er sin' they laid that curst restriction
        On AQUAVITAE;
An' rouse them up to strong conviction,
          An' move their pity.

Stand forth and tell yon PREMIER YOUTH
The honest, open, naked truth;
Tell him o' mine an' Scotland's drouth,
        His servants humble:
The muckle devil blaw you south,
          If ye dissemble!

Does ony *great man* glunch an' gloom?
Speak out an' never fash your thumb!
Let *posts* an' *pensions* sink or swoom
        Wi' them wha grant them:
If honestly they canna come,
          Far better want them.

In gath'rin votes ye were na slack,
Now stand as tightly by your tack:
Ne'er claw your lug, an' fidge your back,
        An' hum an' haw,
But raise your arm, an' tell your crack
          Before them a'.

Paint Scotland greetan owre her thrissle;
Her *mutchkin stowp* as toom's a whissle;
An' damn'd Excise-men in a bussle,
          Seizan a *Stell*,
Triumphant crushan't like a muscle
          Or laimpet shell.

Then on the tither hand present her,
A blackguard *Smuggler*, right behint her,
An', cheek-for-chow, a chuffie *Vintner*,
          Colleaguing join,—
Picking her pouch as bare as Winter,
          Of a' kind coin.

Is there, that bears the name o' SCOT,
But feels his heart's bluid rising hot,
To see his poor, auld Mither's *pot*,
          Thus dung in staves;
An' plunder'd o' her hindmost groat,
          By gallows knaves?

Alas! I'm but a nameless wight,
Trode i' the mire out o' sight!
But could I like MONTGOMERIES fight,
          Or gab like BOSWEL,
There's some *sark-necks* I wad *draw* tight,
          An' *tye* some *hose* well.

God bless your Honors, can ye see't,
The kind, auld, cantie Carlin greet,
An' no get warmly to your feet,
         An' gar them hear it,
An' tell them, wi' a patriot-heat,
         Ye winna bear it?

Some o' you nicely ken the laws,
To round the period an' pause,
An' with rhetoric clause on clause
         To mak harangues;
Then echo thro' Saint Stephen's wa's
         Auld Scotland's wrangs.

Dempster, a true-blue Scot I'se warran;
Thee, aith-detesting, chaste *Kilkerran*;
An' that glib-gabbet Highlan Baron,
         The Laird o' *Graham*;
And ane, a chap that's damn'd auldfarran,
         Dundass his name.

Erskine, a spunkie norland billie;
True Campbels, *Frederic* an' *Ilay*;
An' Livistone, the bauld *Sir Willie*;
         An' mony ithers,
Whom auld Demosthenes or Tully
         Might own for brithers.

Arouse my boys! exert your mettle,
To get auld Scotland back her *kettle*!
Or faith! I'll wad my new pleugh-pettle,
      Ye'll see't or lang,
She'll teach you, wi' a reekan whittle,
      Anither sang.

This while she's been in crankous mood,
Her *lost Militia* fir'd her bluid;
(Deil na they never mair do guid,
      Play'd her that pliskie!)
An' now she's like to rin red-wud
      About her *Whisky*.

An' Lord! if ance they pit her till't,
Her tartan petticoat she'll kilt,
An' durk an' pistol at her belt,
      She'll tak the streets,
An' rin her whittle to the hilt,
      I' th' first she meets!

For God-sake, Sirs! then speak her fair,
An' straik her cannie wi' the hair,
An' to the *muckle house* repair,
      Wi' instant speed,
An' strive, wi' a' your Wit an' Lear,
      To get remead.

Yon ill-tongu'd tinkler, *Charlie Fox*,
May taunt you wi' his jeers an' mocks;
But gie him't het, my hearty cocks!
        E'en cowe the cadie!
An' send him to his dicing box,
        An' sportin lady.

Tell yon guid bluid o' auld *Boconnock*'s,
I'll be his debt twa mashlum bonnocks,
An' drink his health in auld *Nance Tinnock*'s [2]
        Nine times a week,
If he some scheme, like tea an' winnocks,
        Wad kindly seek.

Could he some *commutation* broach,
I'll pledge my aith in guid braid Scotch,
He need na fear their foul reproach
        Nor erudition,
Yon mixtie-maxtie, queer hotch-potch,
        The *Coalition*.

Auld Scotland has a raucle tongue;
She's just a devil wi' a rung;
An' if she promise auld or young
        To tak their part,
Tho' by the neck she should be strung,
        She'll no desert.

[2] A worthy old Hostess of the Author's in *Mauchline*, where he sometimes studies Politics over a glass of guid auld *Scotch Drink*.

And now, ye chosen FIVE AND FORTY,
May still your Mither's heart support ye;
Then tho' a *Minister* grow dorty,
   An' kick your place,
Ye'll snap your fingers, poor an' hearty,
   Before his face.

God bless your Honors, a' your days,
Wi' sowps o' kail an' brats o' claise,
In spite of a' the thievish kaes
   That haunt St *Jamie*'s!
Your humble Bardie sings an' prays
   While *Rab* his name is.

   POSTSCRIPT
Let half-starv'd slaves in warmer skies,
See future wines, rich-clust'ring, rise;
Their lot auld Scotland ne'er envies,
   But blyth an' frisky,
She eyes her freeborn, martial boys,
   Tak aff their Whisky.

What tho' their Phebus kinder warms,
While Fragrance blooms and Beauty charms!
When wretches range, in famish'd swarms,
   The scented groves,
Or hounded forth, *dishonor* arms,
   In hungry droves.

Their *gun*'s a burden on their shouther;
They downa bide the stink o' *powther*;
Their bauldest thought's a hank'ring swither,
        To stan' or rin,
Till skelp—a shot—they're aff, a' throu'ther,
        To save their skin.

But bring a SCOTCHMAN frae his hill,
Clap in his cheek a *highlan gill*,
Say, such is royal GEORGE's will,
        An' there's the foe,
He has nae thought but how to kill
        Twa at a blow.

Nae cauld, faint-hearted doubtings tease him;
Death comes, with fearless eye he sees him;
Wi' bluidy hand a welcome gies him;
        An' when he fa's,
His latest draught o' breathin lea'es him
        In faint huzzas.

Sages their solemn een may steek,
An' raise a philosophic reek,
An' physically causes seek,
        In *clime* an' *season*,
But tell me *Whisky*'s name in Greek,
        I'll tell the reason.

Scotland, my auld, respected Mither!
Tho' whyles ye moistify your leather,
Till when ye speak, ye aiblins blether;
          Yet deil-mak-matter!
Freedom and Whisky gang thegither,
          Tak aff you whitter.

'Love and Liberty' is the ultimate secular cantata, set in an Ayrshire pub. A sequence of separate movements corralled into a spirited chamber piece, it might be considered a close relation of Bach's *Peasant Cantata*, which features a pair of singers on their way to an inn and plays with notions of rustic accents. In its dramatic structure, the poem owes something to the musical form, but Burns politicises the conditions of these jolly beggars in a way that must have seemed shocking when it was eventually published in 1799. A touch of France hangs over the smoky parlour and that final chorus:

> A fig for those by law protected!
> LIBERTY's a glorious feast!
> Courts for Cowards were erected,
> Churches built to please the PRIEST.

Love and Liberty—A Cantata

When lyart leaves bestrow the yird,
Or wavering like the Bauckie-bird,[1]
  Bedim cauld Boreas' blast;
When hailstanes drive wi' bitter skyte,
And infant Frosts begin to bite,
  In hoary cranreuch drest;
Ae night at e'en a merry core
  O' randie, gangrel bodies,
In Poosie-Nansie's[2] held the splore,
  To drink their orra dudies·
Wi' quaffing, and laughing,
  They ranted an' they sang;
Wi' jumping, an' thumping,
  The vera girdle rang.

First, neist the fire, in auld, red rags,
Ane sat; weel brac'd wi' mealy bags,
  And knapsack a' in order;
His doxy lay within his arm;
Wi' USQUEBAE an' blankets warm,
  She blinket on her Sodger:
An' ay he gies the tozie drab
  The tither skelpan kiss,
While she held up her greedy gab,
  Just like an aumous dish:

[1] The old Scotch name for the Bat.
[2] The Hostess of a noted Caravansary in Mauchline, well known to and much frequented by the lowest orders of Travellers and Pilgrims.

Ilk smack still, did crack still,
  Just like a cadger's whip;
Then staggering, an' swaggering,
  He roar'd this ditty up—

AIR

I am a Son of Mars who have been in many wars,
  And show my cuts and scars wherever I come;
This here was for a wench, and that other in a trench,
  When welcoming the French at the sound of the drum.
            Lal de daudle, &c.

My Prenticeship I past where my LEADER breath'd his last,
  When the bloody die was cast on the heights of ABRAM;
And I served out my TRADE when the gallant *game* was play'd,
  And the MORO low was laid at the sound of the drum.

I lastly was with Curtis among the *floating batt'ries*,
  And there I left for witness, an arm and a limb;
Yet let my Country need me, with ELLIOT to head me,
  I'd clatter on my stumps at the sound of a drum.

And now tho' I must beg, with a wooden arm and leg,
  And many a tatter'd rag hanging over my bum,
I'm as happy with my wallet, my bottle and my Callet,
  As when I us'd in scarlet to follow a drum.

What tho', with hoary locks, I must stand the winter shocks,
　　Beneath the woods and rocks oftentimes for a home,
When the tother bag I sell and the tother bottle tell,
　　I could meet a troop of HELL at the sound of a drum.

RECITATIVO

He ended; and the kebars sheuk,
　　Aboon the chorus roar;
While frighted rattons backward leuk,
　　An' seek the benmost bore:
A fairy FIDDLER frae the neuk,
　　He skirl'd out, ENCORE.
But up arose the martial CHUCK,
　　An' laid the loud uproar—

AIR

I once was a Maid, tho' I cannot tell when,
And still my delight is in proper young men:
Some one of a troop of DRAGOONS was my dadie,
No wonder I'm fond of a SODGER LADDIE,
　　　　Sing lal de lal, &c.

The first of my LOVES was a swaggering blade,
To rattle the thundering drum was his trade;
His leg was so tight and his cheek was so ruddy,
Transported I was with my SODGER LADDIE.

But the godly old Chaplain left him in the lurch,
The sword I forsook for the sake of the church;
He ventur'd the SOUL, and I risked the BODY,
'Twas then I prov'd false to my SODGER LADDIE.

Full soon I grew sick of my sanctified *Sot*,
The Regiment AT LARGE for a HUSBAND I got;
From the gilded SPONTOON to the FIFE I was ready;
I asked no more but a SODGER LADDIE.

But the PEACE it reduc'd me to beg in despair,
Till I met my old boy in a CUNNINGHAM fair;
His RAGS REGIMENTAL they flutter'd so gaudy,
My heart it rejoic'd at a SODGER LADDIE.

And now I have liv'd—I know not how long,
And still I can join in a cup and a song;
But whilst with both hands I can hold the glass steady,
Here's to thee, MY HERO, MY SODGER LADDIE.

RECITATIVO
Poor Merry-andrew, in the neuk,
    Sat guzzling wi' a Tinkler-hizzie;
They mind't na wha the chorus teuk,
    Between themsels they were sae busy:
At length wi' drink an' courting dizzy,
    He stoiter'd up an' made a face;
Then turn'd, an' laid a smack on Grizzie,
    Syne tun'd his pipes wi' grave grimace.

Sir Wisdom's a fool when he's fou;
  Sir Knave is a fool in a Session,
He's there but a prentice, I trow,
  But I am a fool by profession.

My Grannie she bought me a beuk,
  An' I held awa to the school;
I fear I my talent misteuk,
  But what will ye hae of a fool.

For drink I would venture my neck;
  A hizzie's the half of my Craft:
But what could ye other expect
  Of ane that's avowedly daft.

I, ance, was ty'd up like a stirk,
  For civilly swearing and quaffing;
I, ance, was abus'd i' the kirk,
  For towsing a lass i' my daffin.

Poor Andrew that tumbles for sport,
  Let nae body name wi' a jeer;
There's even, I'm tauld, i' the Court
  A Tumbler ca'd the Premier.

Observ'd ye yon reverend lad
  Mak faces to tickle the Mob;
He rails at our mountebank squad,
  Its rivalship just i' the job.

And now my conclusion I'll tell,
  For faith I'm confoundedly dry:
The chiel that's a fool for himsel,
  Guid Lord, he's far dafter than I.

RECITATIVO
  Then niest outspak a raucle Carlin,
  Wha ken't fu' weel to cleek the Sterlin;
  For mony a pursie she had hooked,
  An' had in mony a well been douked:
  Her LOVE had been a HIGHLAND LADDIE,
  But weary fa' the waefu' woodie!
  Wi' sighs an' sobs she thus began
  To wail her braw JOHN HIGHLANDMAN—

AIR
A HIGHLAND lad my Love was born,
The lalland laws he held in scorn;
But he still was faithfu' to his clan,
My gallant, braw JOHN HIGHLANDMAN.

CHORUS
  Sing hey my braw John Highlandman!
  Sing ho my braw John Highlandman!
  There's not a lad in a' the lan'
  Was match for my John Highlandman.

With his Philibeg, an' tartan Plaid,
An' guid Claymore down by his side,
The ladies' hearts he did trepan,
My gallant, braw John Highlandman.
   Sing hey, &c.

We ranged a' from Tweed to Spey,
An' liv'd like lords an' ladies gay:
For a lalland face he feared none,
My gallant, braw John Highlandman.
   Sing hey, &c.

They banish'd him beyond the sea,
But ere the bud was on the tree,
Adown my cheeks the pearls ran,
Embracing my John Highlandman.
   Sing hey, &c.

But Och! they catch'd him at the last,
And bound him in a dungeon fast,
My curse upon them every one,
They've hang'd my braw John Highlandman.
   Sing hey, &c.

And now a Widow I must mourn
The Pleasures that will ne'er return;
No comfort but a hearty can,
When I think on John Highlandman.
   Sing hey, &c.

A pigmy Scraper wi' his Fiddle,
Wha us'd to trystes an' fairs to driddle,
Her strappan limb an' gausy middle,
      (He reach'd nae higher)
Had hol'd his HEARTIE like a riddle,
      An' blawn't on fire.

Wi' hand on hainch, and upward e'e,
He croon'd his gamut, ONE, TWO, THREE,
Then in an ARIOSO key,
      The wee Apollo
Set off wi' ALLEGRETTO glee
      His GIGA SOLO——

AIR
Let me ryke up to dight that tear,
An' go wi' me an' be my DEAR;
An' then your every CARE an' FEAR
May whistle owre the lave o't.

CHORUS
I am a Fiddler to my trade,
An' a' the tunes that e'er I play'd,
The sweetest still to WIFE or MAID,
Was whistle owre the lave o't.

At KIRNS an' WEDDINS we'se be there,
An' O sae nicely's we will fare!
We'll bowse about till Dadie CARE
  Sing whistle owre the lave o't.
        I am, &c.

Sae merrily's the banes we'll pyke,
An' sun oursells about the dyke;
An' at our leisure when ye like
  We'll whistle owre the lave o't.
        I am, &c.

But bless me wi' your heav'n o' charms,
An' while I kittle hair on thairms
HUNGER, CAULD, an' a' sic harms
  May whistle owre the lave o't.
        I am, &c.

RECITATIVO

Her charms had struck a sturdy CAIRD,
  As weel as poor GUTSCRAPER;
He taks the Fiddler by the beard,
  An' draws a roosty rapier—
He swoor by a' was swearing worth
  To speet him like a Pliver,
Unless he would from that time forth
  Relinquish her for ever:

Wi' ghastly e'e poor TWEEDLEDEE
  Upon his hunkers bended,
An' pray'd for grace wi' ruefu' face,
  An' so the quarrel ended;
But tho' his little heart did grieve,
  When round the TINKLER prest her,
He feign'd to snirtle in his sleeve
  When thus the CAIRD address'd her—

AIR

My bonie lass, I work in brass,
  A TINKLER is my station;
I've travell'd round all Christian ground
  In this my occupation;
I've ta'en the gold an' been enroll'd
  In many a noble squadron;
But vain they search'd when off I march'd
  To go an' clout the CAUDRON.
        I've taen the gold, &c.

Despise that SHRIMP, that withered IMP,
  With a' his noise an' cap'rin;
An' take a share, with those that bear
  The *budget* and the *apron*!
And *by* that STOWP! my faith an' houpe,
  And *by* that dear KILBAIGIE,[3]
If e'er ye want, or meet with scant,
  May I ne'er weet my CRAIGIE!
        And by that Stowp, &c.

[3] A peculiar sort of Whiskie so called: a great favourite with Poosie Nansie's Clubs.

The Caird prevail'd—th' unblushing fair
  In his embraces sunk;
Partly wi' LOVE o'ercome sae sair,
  An' partly she was drunk:
SIR VIOLINO with an air,
  That show'd a man o' spunk,
Wish'd UNISON between the PAIR,
  An' made the bottle clunk
        To their health that night.

But hurchin Cupid shot a shaft,
  That play'd a DAME a shavie—
The Fiddler RAK'D her, FORE AND AFT,
  Behint the Chicken cavie:
Her lord, a wight of HOMER's craft,[4]
  Tho' limpan wi' the Spavie,
He hirpl'd up an' lap like daft,
  An' shor'd them DAINTY DAVIE
        O' *boot* that night.

He was a care-defying blade,
  As ever BACCHUS listed!
Tho' Fortune sair upon him laid,
  His heart she ever miss'd it.
He had no WISH but—to be glad,
  Nor WANT but—when he thristed;
He hated nought but—to be sad,
An' thus the Muse suggested
        His sang that night.

[4] Homer is allowed to be the eldest Ballad singer on record.

I am a BARD of no regard,
  Wi' gentle folks an' a' that;
But HOMER LIKE the glowran byke,
  Frae town to town I draw that.

CHORUS

  For a' that an' a' that,
    An' twice as muckle's a' that,
  I've lost but ANE, I've TWA behin',
  I've WIFE ENEUGH for a' that.

I never drank the Muses' STANK,
  Castalia's burn an' a' that,
But there it streams an' richly reams,
  My HELICON I ca' that.
        For a' that, &c.

Great love I bear to all the FAIR,
  Their humble slave and a' that;
But lordly WILL, I hold it still
  A mortal sin to thraw that.
        For a' that, &c.

In raptures sweet this hour we meet,
  Wi' mutual love an' a' that;
But for how lang the FLIE MAY STANG,
  Let INCLINATION law that.
        For a' that, &c.

Their tricks an' craft hae put me daft,
  They've ta'en me in, an' a' that,
But clear your decks an' here's the SEX!
  I like the jads for a' that.
    For a' that an' a' that
      An' twice as muckle's a' that,
    My DEAREST BLUID to do them guid,
      They're welcome till't for a' that.

          RECITATIVO

So sang the BARD—and Nansie's waws
Shook with a thunder of applause
  Re-echo'd from each mouth!
They toom'd their pocks, they pawn'd their duds,
They scarcely left to coor their fuds
  To quench their lowan drouth:
Then owre again the jovial thrang
  The Poet did request
To lowse his PACK an' wale a sang,
  A BALLAD o' the best.
    He, rising, rejoicing,
      Between his TWA DEBORAHS,
    Looks round him an' found them
      Impatient for the Chorus.

             AIR

See the smoking bowl before us,
  Mark our jovial, ragged ring!
Round and round take up the Chorus,
  And in raptures let us sing—

A fig for those by law protected!
 LIBERTY's a glorious feast!
Courts for Cowards were erected,
 Churches built to please the PRIEST.

What is TITLE, what is TREASURE,
 What is REPUTATION's care?
If we lead a life of pleasure,
 'Tis no matter HOW or WHERE.
     A fig, &c.

With the ready trick and fable
 Round we wander all the day;
And at night, in barn or stable,
 Hug our doxies on the hay.
     A fig, &c.

Does the train-attended CARRIAGE
 Thro' the country lighter rove?
Does the sober bed of MARRIAGE
 Witness brighter scenes of love?
     A fig, &c.

Life is al a VARIORUM,
 We regard not how it goes;
Let them cant about DECORUM,
 Who have character to lose.
     A fig, &c.

Here's to Budgets, Bags and Wallets!
  Here's to all the wandering train!
Here's our ragged Brats and Callets!
  One and all cry out, Amen!
    A fig for those by Law protected,
      Liberty's a glorious feast!
    Courts for Cowards were erected,
      Churches built to please the Priest.

Our poet suffered many insults to his freedom as a writer, perhaps none so exhausting as having to supplement the farm income by working for the Excise. The best of his biographers, Catherine Carswell, writes beautifully of Burns at the moment of capture: 'Pledged to subserviency as a petty official, like a man in a nightmare, helpless but exquisitely sentient, he watched the Muses waving their mocking farewell from a far distance.' Burns's health was ruined by his labours for the Tax: long days and comfortless journeys on horseback, soaked to the skin as he checked the contents of old women's barrels, he hated a job so meanly rigged against his best instincts, drawing an annual percentage from the joys of life.

The Deil's Awa wi' the Exciseman

The deil cam fiddlin thro' the town,
  And danc'd awa wi' th' Exciseman;
And ilka wife cries, auld Mahoun,
  I wish you luck o' the prize, man.

CHORUS
The deil's awa, the deil's awa,
  The deil's awa wi' th' Exciseman,
He's danc'd awa, he's danc'd awa,
  He's danc'd awa wi' th' Exciseman.

We'll mak our maut and we'll brew our drink,
  We'll laugh, sing, and rejoice, man;
And mony braw thanks to the meikle black deil,
  That danc'd awa wi' th' Exciseman.
        The deil's awa, &c.

There's threesome reels, there's foursome reels,
  There's hornpipes and strathspeys, man,
But the ae best dance e'er cam to the Land
  Was, the deil's awa wi' th' Exciseman.
        The deil's awa, &c.

You'll never find a better song to be sung by a trio of drunks than 'Willie Brew'd a Peck o' Maut'. The song can actually make you thirsty for a drink, and even more for a blind night in the company of the like-minded. The moon sits blinking in the 'lift', a right good word for the sky, and a word well used more than a hundred years later in the lyrics of Hugh MacDiarmid, whose drunk man looking at the thistle might have fallen through the years to bump down with the sort of hangover brewed by Willie's malt.

Willie Brew'd a Peck o' Maut

O Willie brew'd a peck o' maut,
  And Rob and Allan cam to see;
Three blyther hearts, that lee lang night,
  Ye wad na found in Christendie.

CHORUS
We are na fou, we're nae that fou,
  But just a drappie in our e'e;
The cock may craw, the day may daw,
  And ay we'll taste the barley bree.

Here are we met, three merry boys,
  Three merry boys I trow are we;
And mony a night we've merry been,
  And mony mae we hope to be!
      We are na fou, &c.

It is the moon, I ken her horn,
  That's blinkin in the lift sae hie;
She shines sae bright to wyle us hame,
  But by my sooth she'll wait a wee!
      We are na fou, &c.

Wha first shall rise to gang awa,
  A cuckold, coward loun is he!
Wha first beside his chair shall fa',
  He is the king amang us three!
      We are na fou, &c.

The last three minutes of the old year and the first two minutes of the new one provide a caesura of pure sentiment in the average Scots household: a perfectly encapsulated delirium of happy sadness and lost time. When I think back over nearly forty of those five-minute intervals, I see a procession of departed relatives and rosy-cheeked First Foots – coal in hand, whisky bottle under the arm, tears forming in the corners of eyes – waiting at the front door to grasp a hand and take a cup of kindness. One year, an old gentleman called Robbie Proudfoot came to the house. A recovering alcoholic from a village near Stranraer, he stood in our living-room with a glass of dandelion-and-burdock and toasted all the handsome drinks – 'the right gude-willie-waught' – of former days and we drove through the snow to a hall in Irvine. In that Drill Hall stood all the recovering alcoholics of Ayrshire, passing those dangerous hours after the Bells in the company of one another, and they danced and sang in an absence of drink. It happened a long time ago, as did everything in its turn, and 'Auld Lang Syne' brings the colour of those nights back to life, a song with a precise gift for mellowing our regrets and putting out a hand to all that is human and passing.

Auld Lang Syne

Should auld acquaintance be forgot
  And never brought to mind?
Should auld acquaintance be forgot,
  And auld lang syne!

For auld lang syne, my jo,
  For auld lang syne,
We'll tak a cup o' kindness yet
  For auld lang syne.

And surely ye'll be your pint stowp!
  And surely I'll be mine!
And we'll tak a cup o' kindness yet,
  For auld lang syne.
            For auld, &c.

We twa hae run about the braes,
  And pou'd the gowans fine;
But we've wander'd mony a weary fitt,
  Sin auld lang syne.
            For auld, &c.

We twa hae paidl'd in the burn,
  Frae morning sun till dine;
But seas between us braid hae roar'd,
  Sin auld lang syne.
        For auld, &c.

And there's a hand, my trusty fiere!
  And gie's a hand o' thine!
And we'll tak a right gude-willie-waught,
  For auld lang syne.
        For auld, &c.

If nobody restrains us, we will drink ourselves to destruction. Apart from the Russians and Scandinavians, I know of no people so dedicated as the British to stupefying themselves with alcohol.

Hogarth's biting depiction of Gin Lane and Cruickshank's great anti-alcohol paintings are there to remind us of the hoggish, violent and self-destructive state we get into when we can, and the trail of wreckage we leave in broken marriages, neglected children and destroyed lives.

Peter Hitchins, *Daily Mail*, April 2004

Address to the Unco Guid, or the Rigidly Righteous

My Son, these maxims make a rule,
  And lump them ay thegither;
The Rigid Righteous *is a fool,*
  The Rigid Wise *anither:*
The cleanest corn that e'er was dight
  May hae some pyles o' caff in;
So ne'er a fellow-creature slight
  For random fits o' daffin.
                    Solomon——Eccles., vii:16

O ye wha are sae guid yoursel,
  Sae pious and sae holy,
Ye've nought to do but mark and tell
  Your Neebours' fauts and folly!
Whase life is like a weel-gaun mill,
  Supply'd wi' store o' water,
The heaped happer's ebbing still,
  And still the clap plays clatter.

Hear me, ye venerable Core,
  As counsel for poor mortals,
That frequent pass douce Wisdom's door
  For glaikit Folly's portals;
I, for their thoughtless, careless sakes
  Would here propone defences,
Their donsie tricks, their black mistakes,
  Their failings and mischances.

Ye see your state wi' theirs compar'd,
  And shudder at the niffer,
But cast a moment's fair regard
  What maks the mighty differ;
Discount what scant occasion gave,
  That purity ye pride in,
And (what's aft mair than a' the lave)
  Your better art o' hiding.

Think, when your castigated pulse
  Gies now and then a wallop,
What ragings must his veins convulse,
  That still eternal gallop:
Wi' wind and tide fair i' your tail,
  Right on ye scud your sea-way;
But, in the teeth o' baith to sail,
  It maks an unco leeway.

See Social-life and Glee sit down,
  All joyous and unthinking,
Till, quite transmugrify'd, they're grown
  Debauchery and Drinking:
O would they stay to calculate
  Th' eternal consequences;
Or your more dreaded hell to state,
  Damnation of expences!

Ye high, exalted, virtuous Dames,
  Ty'd up in godly laces,
Before ye gie poor *Frailty* names,
  Suppose a change o' cases;
A dear-lov'd lad, convenience snug,
  A treacherous inclination—
But, let me whisper i' your lug,
  Ye're aiblins nae temptation.

Then gently scan your brother Man,
  Still gentler sister Woman;
Tho' they may gang a kennin wrang,
  To step aside is human:
One point must still be greatly dark,
  The moving *Why* they do it;
And just as lamely can ye mark,
  How far perhaps they rue it.

Who made the heart, 'tis *He* alone
  Decidedly can try us,
He knows each chord its various tone,
  Each spring its various bias:
Then at the balance let's be mute,
  We never can adjust it;
What's *done* we partly may compute,
  But know not what's *resisted*.

The Immortals

The Ayrshire fiction-writer John Galt — Coleridge's favourite novelist — must have got the idea of the pawky, double-dealing minister from Burns, for in *Annals of the Parish* he presents a man totally relentless in his scraping manners and his pantomimic piety. The combination is native to Holy Willie, who reminds us that self-abasement is merely the queasier partner of personal ambition. Galt's satire has the warm colours of the Flemish masters; so does Burns's portrait of Holy Willie, whose roseate face and watery eye we might imagine peeping over a guttering candle flame.

Holy Willie's Prayer

And send the godly in a pet to pray—

Pope

ARGUMENT

Holy Willie was a rather oldish bachelor Elder in the parish of Mauchline, and much and justly famed for that polemical chattering which ends in tippling Orthodoxy, and for that Spiritualized Bawdry which refines to Liquorish Devotion.—
In a Sessional process with a gentleman in Mauchline, a Mr Gavin Hamilton, Holy Willie, and his priest, father Auld, after full hearing in the Presbytry of Ayr, came off but second best; owing partly to the oratorical powers of Mr Robert Aiken, Mr Hamilton's Counsel; but chiefly to Mr Hamilton's being one of the most irreproachable and truly respectable characters in the country.—On losing his Process, the Muse overheard him at his devotions as follows—

O Thou that in the heavens does dwell!
Wha, as it pleases best Thysel,
Sends ane to heaven and ten to hell,
  A' for Thy glory!
And no for ony gude or ill
  They've done before Thee.—

I bless and praise Thy matchless might,
When thousands Thou has left in night,
That I am here before Thy sight,
        For gifts and grace,
A burning and a shining light
        To a' this place.—

What was I, or my generation,
That I should get such exaltation?
I, wha deserv'd most just damnation,
        For broken laws
Sax thousand years ere my creation,
        Thro' Adam's cause!

When from my mother's womb I fell,
Thou might hae plunged me deep in hell,
To gnash my gooms, and weep, and wail,
        In burning lakes,
Where damned devils roar and yell
        Chain'd to their stakes.—

Yet I am here, a chosen sample,
To shew Thy grace is great and ample:
I'm here, a pillar o' Thy temple
        Strong as a rock,
A guide, a ruler and example
        To a' Thy flock.—

O Lord Thou kens what zeal I bear,
When drinkers drink, and swearers swear,
And singin' there, and dancin' here,
            Wi' great an' sma';
For I am keepet by Thy fear,
            Free frae them a'.—

But yet—O Lord—confess I must—
At times I'm fash'd wi' fleshly lust;
And sometimes too, in warldly trust
            Vile Self gets in;
But Thou remembers we are dust,
            Defil'd wi' sin.—

O Lord—yestreen—Thou kens—wi' Meg—
Thy pardon I sincerely beg!
O may't ne'er be a living plague,
            To my dishonor!
And I'll ne'er lift a lawless leg
            Again upon her.—

Besides, I farther maun avow,
Wi' Leezie's lass, three times—I trow—
But Lord, that friday I was fou
            When I cam near her;
Or else, Thou kens, Thy servant true
            Wad never steer her.—

Maybe Thou lets this fleshy thorn
Buffet Thy servant e'en and morn,
Lest he o'er proud and high should turn,
   That he's sae gifted;
If sae, Thy hand maun e'en be borne
   Untill Thou lift it.—

Lord bless Thy Chosen in this place,
For here Thou has a chosen race:
But God, confound their stubborn face,
   And blast their name,
Wha bring Thy rulers to disgrace
   And open shame.—

Lord mind Gaun Hamilton's deserts!
He drinks, and swears, and plays at cartes,
Yet has sae mony taking arts
   Wi' Great and Sma',
Frae God's ain priest the people's hearts
   He steals awa.—

And when we chasten'd him therefore,
Thou kens how he bred sic a splore,
And set the warld in a roar
   O' laughin at us:
Curse Thou his basket and his store,
   Kail and potatoes.—

Lord hear my earnest cry and prayer
Against that Presbytry of Ayr!
Thy strong right hand, Lord, make it bare
          Upon their heads!
Lord visit them, and dinna spare,
          For their misdeeds!

O Lord my God, that glib-tongu'd Aiken!
My very heart and flesh are quaking
To think how I sat, sweating, shaking,
          And piss'd wi' dread,
While Auld wi' hingin lip gaed sneaking
          And hid his head.

Lord, in Thy day o' vengeance try him!
Lord visit him that did employ him!
And pass not in Thy mercy by them,
          Nor hear their prayer;
But for Thy people's sake destroy them,
          And dinna spare!

But Lord, remember me and mine
Wi' mercies temporal and divine!
That I for grace and gear may shine,
          Excell'd by nane!
And a' the glory shall be Thine!
          AMEN! AMEN!

Heresy is a model of resistance in the mind of a free man. That is perhaps why Burns admired Milton's Satan, his 'manly fortitude in supporting what cannot be remedied – in short, the wild broken fragments of a noble mind, exalted in ruins'. Burns was careless with the Kirk authorities, but good relations between literature and laughter must often depend on an author's willingness to endure the penalties of public disgrace.

The Kirk of Scotland's Garland—A New Song

Orthodox, Orthodox, who believe in John Knox,
   Let me sound an alarm to your conscience;
A heretic blast has been blawn i' the West—
   That what is not Sense must be Nonsense, Orthodox,
   That what is not Sense must be Nonsense.—

Doctor Mac, Doctor Mac, ye should streek on a rack,
   To strike Evildoers with terror;
To join FAITH and SENSE upon any pretence
   Was heretic, damnable error, &c.

Town of Ayr, Town of Ayr, it was rash, I declare,
   To meddle wi' mischief a brewing;
Provost John is still deaf to the Church's relief,
   And Orator Bob is its ruin, &c.

D'rymple mild, D'rymple mild, tho' your heart's like a child,
   And your life like the new-driven snaw;
Yet that winna save ye, auld Satan maun have ye,
   For preaching that three's ane and twa, &c.

Calvin's Sons, Calvin's Sons, seize your spiritual guns—
   Ammunition ye never can need;
Your HEARTS are the stuff will be POWDER enough,
   And your SCULLS are a storehouse o' LEAD, &c.

Rumble John, Rumble John, mount the steps with a groan,
  Cry, the Book is with heresy cramm'd;
Then lug out your ladle, deal brimstone like aidle,
  And roar ev'ry note o' the Damn'd, &c.

Simper James, Simper James, leave the fair Killie dames,
  There's a holier chase in your view:
I'll lay on your head that the Pack ye'll soon lead,
  For Puppies like you there's but few, &c.

Singet Sawnie, Singet Sawnie, are ye herding the Pennie,
  Unconscious what danger awaits?
With a jump, yell and howl, alarm ev'ry soul,
  For Hannibal's just at your gates, &c.

Poet Willie, Poet Willie, gie the Doctor a volley
  Wi' your 'liberty's chain' and your wit:
O'er Pegasus' side ye ne'er laid a stride,
  Ye only stood by where he shit, &c.

Andrew Gowk, Andrew Gowk, ye may slander the Book,
  And the Book nought the waur, let me tell ye:
Ye're rich and look big, but lay by hat and wig—
  And ye'll hae a Calf's-head o' sma' value, &c.

Barr Steenie, Barr Steenie, what mean ye, what mean ye?
  If ye'll meddle nae mair wi' the matter,
Ye may hae some pretence, man, to havins and sense, man,—
  Wi' people that ken you nae better, &c.

Jamie Goose, Jamie Goose, ye hae made but toom roose
  O' hunting the wicked Lieutenant;
But the Doctor's your mark, for the Lord's holy ark
  He has couper'd and ca'd a wrang pin in, &c.

Davie Rant, Davie Rant, wi' a face like a saunt,
  And a heart that wad poison a hog;
Raise an impudent roar, like a breaker lee-shore,
  Or the KIRK will be tint in a bog, &c.

Cessnock-side, Cessnock-side, wi' your turkey-cock pride,
  O' manhood but sma' is your share;
Ye've the figure, it's true, even your faes maun allow,
  And your friends dare na say ye hae mair, &c.

Muirland Jock, Muirland Jock, whom the Lord made a rock
  To crush Common sense for her sins;
If ill-manners were Wit, there's no mortal so fit
  To confound the poor Doctor at ance, &c.

Daddie Auld, Daddie Auld, there'a a tod i' the fauld,
  A tod meikle waur than the CLERK:
Tho' ye do little skaith ye'll be in at the death,
  For if ye canna bite ye can bark, &c.

Holy Will, Holy Will, there was wit i' your skull,
  When ye pilfer'd the alms o' the poor;
The timmer is scant, when ye're ta'en for a saint,
  Wha should swing in a rape for an hour, &c.

Poet Burns, Poet Burns, wi' your priest-skelping turns,
   Why desert ye your auld native shire?
Tho' your Muse is a gipsey, yet were she even tipsey,
   She could ca' us nae waur than we are, Poet Burns,
   She could ca' us nae waur than we are.—

With a true poet, sedition may show itself in the metre, and Burns knew best of all how to breathe liberal philosophy into the rhythm of his lines. Fundamentalism's iron rhetoric may yield to nothing but the softness of flesh, but here is sensuality and humour in a poem. And that may be counted among Burns's secrets: he gives life to fairness by discovering the roots of its sound.

The Holy Fair

A robe of seeming truth and trust
  Hid crafty Observation;
And secret hung, with poison'd crust,
  The dirk of Defamation:
A mask that like the gorget show'd,
  Dye-varying, on the pigeon;
And for a mantle large and broad,
  He wrapt him in Religion.——

              Hypocrisy a-la-Mode

Upon a simmer *Sunday morn*,
  When Nature's face is fair,
I walked forth to view the corn,
  An' snuff the callor air:
The rising sun, owre GALSTON muirs,
  Wi' glorious light was glintan;
The hares were hirplan down the furrs,
  The lav'rocks they were chantan
              Fu' sweet that day.

As lightsomely I glowr'd abroad,
  To see a scene sae gay,
Three *hizzies*, early at the road,
  Cam skelpan up the way.
Twa had manteeles o' dolefu' black,
  But ane wi' lyart lining;
The *third*, that gaed a wee aback,
  Was in the fashion shining
              Fu' gay that day.

111

The *twa* appear'd like sisters twin,
  In feature, form, an' claes;
Their visage—wither'd, lang an' thin,
  An' sour as onie slaes:
The *third* cam up, hap-step-an'-loup,
  As light as onie lambie,—
An' wi' a curchie low did stoop,
  As soon as e'er she saw me,
          Fu' kind that day.

Wi' bonnet aff, quoth I, 'Sweet lass,
  I think ye seem to ken me;
I'm sure I've seen that bonie face,
  But yet I canna name ye.—'
Quo' she, an' laughan as she spak,
  An' taks me by the hands,
'Ye, for my sake, hae gien the feck
  Of a' the *ten commands*
          A screed some day.

'My name is FUN—your cronie dear,
  The nearest friend ye hae;
An' this is SUPERSTITION here,
  An' that's HYPOCRISY:
I'm gaun to Mauchline *holy fair*,
  To spend an hour in daffin;
Gin ye'll go there, yon runkl'd pair,
  We will get famous laughin
          At them this day.'

Quoth I, 'With a' my heart, I'll do't;
  I'll get my Sunday's sark on,
An' meet you on the holy spot;
  Faith, we'se hae fine remarkin!'
Then I gaed hame, at crowdie-time,
  An' soon I made me ready;
For roads were clad, frae side to side,
  Wi' monie a weary body,
            In droves that day.

Here, farmers gash, in ridin graith,
  Gaed hoddan by their cotters;
There, swankies young, in braw braid-claith,
  Are springan owre the gutters.
The lasses, skelpan barefit, thrang,
  In silks an' scarlets glitter;
Wi' *sweet-milk cheese*, in mony a whang,
  An' *farls*, bak'd wi' butter,
            Fu' crump that day.

When by the *plate* we set our nose,
  Weel heaped up wi' ha'pence,
A greedy glowr *Black-bonnet* throws,
  An' we maun draw our tippence.
Then in we go to see the show,
  On ev'ry side they're gath'ran;
Some carryan dails, some chairs an' stools,
  An' some are busy bleth'ran
            Right loud that day.

Here, stands a shed to fend the show'rs,
　　An' screen our countra Gentry;
There, *Racer-Jess*, an' twathree whores,
　　Are blinkan at the entry:
Here sits a raw o' tittlan jads,
　　Wi' heaving breasts an' bare neck;
An' there, a batch o' *Wabster lads*,
　　Blackguarding frae Kilmarnock
　　　　　　For *fun* this day.

Here, some are thinkan on their sins,
　　An' some upo' their claes;
Ane curses feet that fyl'd his shins,
　　Anither sighs an' prays:
On this hand sits a Chosen swatch,
　　Wi' screw'd-up, grace-proud faces;
On that, a set o' chaps, at watch,
　　Thrang winkan on the lasses
　　　　　　To *chairs* that day.

O happy is that man, an' blest!
　　Nae wonder that it pride him!
Whase ain dear lass, that he likes best,
　　Comes clinkan down beside him!
Wi' arm repos'd on the *chair back*,
　　He sweetly does compose him;
Which, by degrees, slips round her *neck*,
　　An's loof upon her *bosom*
　　　　　　Unkend that day.

Now a' the congregation o'er,
  Is silent expectation;
For Moodie speels the holy door,
  Wi' tidings o' damnation:
Should *Hornie*, as in ancient days,
  'Mang sons o' God present him,
The vera sight o' Moodie's face,
  To 's ain *het hame* had sent him
         Wi' fright that day.

Hear how he clears the points o' Faith
  Wi' rattlin an' thumpin!
Now meekly calm, now wild in wrath,
  He's stampan, an' he's jumpan!
His lengthen'd chin, his turn'd up snout,
  His eldritch squeel an' gestures,
O how they fire the heart devout,
  Like cantharidian plaisters
         On sic a day!

But hark! the *tent* has chang'd its voice;
  There's peace an' rest nae langer;
For a' the *real judges* rise,
  They canna sit for anger.
Smith opens out his cauld harangues,
  On *practice* and on *morals*;
An' aff the godly pour in thrangs,
  To gie the jars an' barrels
         A lift that day.

What signifies his barren shine,
  Of *moral pow'rs* an' *reason*;
His English style, an' gesture fine,
  Are a' clean out o' season.
Like SOCRATES or ANTONINE,
  Or some auld pagan heathen,
The *moral man* he does define,
  But ne'er a word o' *faith* in
            That's right that day.

In guid time comes an antidote
  Against sic poosion'd nostrum;
For Peebles, frae the water-fit,
  Ascends the *holy rostrum*:
See, up he's got the Word o' God,
  An' meek an' mim has view'd it,
While COMMON-SENSE has taen the road,
  An' aff, an' up the *Cowgate*
            Fast, fast that day.

Wee Miller niest, the Guard relieves,
  An' Orthodoxy raibles,
Tho' in his heart he weel believes,
  An' thinks it auld wives' fables:
But faith! the birkie wants a *Manse*,
  So, cannilie he hums them;
Altho' his *carnal* Wit an' Sense
  Like hafflins-wise o'ercomes him
            At times that day.

Now, butt an' ben, the Change-house fills,
  Wi' *yill-caup* Commentators:
Here's crying out for bakes an' gills,
  An' there, the pint-stowp clatters;
While thick an' thrang, an' loud an' lang,
  Wi' *Logic*, an' wi' *Scripture*,
They raise a din, that, in the end,
  Is like to breed a rupture
        O' wrath that day.

Leeze me on Drink! it gies us mair
  Than either School or Colledge:
It kindles Wit, it waukens Lear,
  It pangs us fou o' Knowledge.
Be't *whisky-gill* or *penny-wheep*,
  Or onie stronger potion,
It never fails, on drinkin deep,
  To kittle up our *notion*,
        By night or day.

The lads an' lasses, blythely bent
  To mind baith *saul* an' *body*,
Sit round the table, weel content,
  An' steer about the *Toddy*.
On this ane's dress, an' that ane's leuk,
  They're makin observations;
While some are cozie i' the neuk,
  An' forming *assignations*
        To meet some day.

But now the Lord's ain trumpet touts,
  Till a' the hills are rairan,
An' echos back return the shouts,
  Black Russell is na spairan:
His piercin words, like highlan swords,
  Divide the joints an' marrow;
His talk o' Hell, whare devils dwell,
  Our vera 'Sauls does harrow'
            Wi' fright that day.

A vast, unbottom'd, boundless *Pit*,
  Fill'd fou o' *lowan brunstane*.
Whase raging flame, an' scorching heat,
  Wad melt the hardest whunstane!
The *half-asleep* start up wi' fear,
  An' think they hear it roaran,
When presently it does appear,
  'Twas but some neebor *snoran*
            Asleep that day.

'Twad be owre lang a tale to tell,
  How monie stories past,
An' how they crouded to the yill,
  When they were a' dismist:
How drink gaed round, in cogs an' caups,
  Amang the furms an' benches;
An' *cheese* an' *bread*, frae women's laps,
  Was dealt about in lunches,
            An' dawds that day.

In comes a gausie, gash *Guidwife*,
　　An' sits down by the fire,
Syn draws her *kebbuck* an' her knife;
　　The lasses they are shyer.
The auld *Guidmen*, about the *grace*,
　　Frae side to side they bother,
Till some ane by his bonnet lays,
　　An' gies them't, like a *tether*,
　　　　　　Fu' lang that day.

Wae sucks! for him that gets nae lass,
　　Or lasses that hae naething!
Sma' need has he to say a grace,
　　Or melvie his braw claething!
O *Wives* be mindfu', ance yoursel,
　　How bonie lads ye wanted,
An' dinna, for a *kebbuck-heel*,
　　Let lasses be affronted
　　　　　　On sic a day!

Now *Clinkumbell*, wi' rattlan tow,
　　Begins to jow an' croon;
Some swagger hame, the best they dow,
　　Some wait the afternoon.
At slaps the billies halt a blink,
　　Till lasses strip their shoon:
Wi' *faith* an' *hope*, an' *love* an' *drink*,
　　They're a' in famous tune
　　　　　　For crack that day.

How monie hearts this day converts,
  O' Sinners and o' Lasses!
Their hearts o' stane, gin night are gane
  As saft as ony flesh is.
There's some are fou o' *love divine*;
  There's some are fou o' *brandy*;
An' monie jobs that day begin,
  May end in *Houghmagandie*
        Some ither day.

A Guy Named Satan

I n one appearance, Boykin [Lieutenant General William G. Boykin, the United States Deputy Undersecretary of Defense for Intelligence] told a religious group in Oregon that Islamic extremists hate the United States 'because we're a Christian nation, because our foundation and our roots are Judeo-Christian . . . And the enemy is a guy named Satan.'

CBS News, August 2004

Address to the Deil

O Prince, O chief of many throned pow'rs,
That led th' embattl'd Seraphim to war—

                              Milton

O thou, whatever title suit thee!
Auld Hornie, Satan, Nick, or Clootie,
Wha in yon cavern grim an' sooty
            Clos'd under hatches,
Spairges about the brunstane cootie,
            To scaud poor wretches!

Hear me, *auld Hangie*, for a wee,
An' let poor, *damned bodies* bee;
I'm sure sma' pleasure it can gie,
            Ev'n to a *deil*,
To skelp an' scaud poor dogs like me,
            An' hear us squeel!

Great is thy pow'r, an' great thy fame;
Far ken'd, an' noted is thy name;
An' tho' yon *lowan heugh*'s thy hame,
            Thou travels far;
An' faith! thou's neither lag nor lame,
            Nor blate nor scaur.

Whyles, ranging like a roaring lion,
For prey, a' holes an' corners tryin;
Whyles, on the strong-wing'd Tempest flyin,
      Tirlan the *kirks*;
Whyles, in the human bosom pryin,
      Unseen thou lurks.

I've heard my rev'rend *Graunie* say,
In lanely glens ye like to stray;
Or where auld, ruin'd castles, gray,
      Nod to the moon,
Ye fright the nightly wand'rer's way,
      Wi' eldritch croon.

When twilight did my *Graunie* summon,
To say her pray'rs, douse, honest woman,
Aft 'yont the dyke she's heard you bumman,
      Wi' eerie drone;
Or, rustling, thro' the boortries coman,
      Wi' heavy groan.

Ae dreary, windy, winter night,
The stars shot down wi' sklentan light,
Wi' you, *mysel*, I gat a fright
      Ayont the lough;
Ye, like a *rash-buss*, stood in sight,
      Wi' wavin' sugh:

The cudgel in my nieve did shake,
Each bristl'd hair stood like a stake,
When wi' an eldritch, stoor, *quaick, quaick,*
   Amang the springs,
Awa ye squatter'd like a *drake,*
   On whistling wings.

Let *Warlocks* grim, an' wither'd *Hags,*
Tell, how wi' you, on ragweed nags,
They skim the muirs an' dizzy crags,
   Wi' wicked speed;
And in kirk-yards renew their leagues,
   Owre howcket dead.

Thence, countra wives, wi' toil an' pain,
May plunge an' plunge the *kirn* in vain;
For Och! the yellow treasure's taen,
   By witching skill;
An' dawtit, twal-pint *Hawkie*'s gane
   As yell's the Bill.

Thence, mystic knots mak great abuse,
On *Young-Guidmen,* fond, keen an' croose;
When the best *warklum* i' the house,
   By cantraip wit,
Is instant made no worth a louse,
   Just at the bit.

When thowes dissolve the snawy hoord,
An' float the jinglan icy boord,
Then, *Water-kelpies* haunt the foord,
   By your direction,
An' nighted Trav'llers are allur'd
   To their destruction.

An' aft your moss-traversing *Spunkies*
Decoy the wight that late an' drunk is;
The bleezan, curst, mischievous monkies
   Delude his eyes,
Till in some miry slough he sunk is,
   Ne'er mair to rise.

When MASONS' mystic *word* an' *grip*,
In storms an' tempests raise you up,
Some cock, or cat, your rage maun stop,
   Or, strange to tell!
The *youngest Brother* ye wad whip
   Aff straught to Hell.

Lang syne in *Eden*'s bonie yard,
When youthfu' lovers first were pair'd,
An' all the Soul of Love they shar'd,
   The raptur'd hour,
Sweet on the fragrant, flow'ry swaird,
   In shady bow'r:

126

Then you, ye auld, snick-drawing dog!
Ye cam to Paradise incog,
An' play'd on a man a cursed brogue,
        (Black be your fa'!)
An' gied the infant warld a shog,
        'Maist ruin'd a'.

D'ye mind that day, when in a bizz,
Wi' reeket duds, an' reestet gizz,
Ye did present your smoutie phiz
        'Mang better folk,
An' sklented on the *man of Uz*
        Your spitefu' joke?

An' how ye gat him i' your thrall,
An' brak him out o' house an' hal',
While scabs an' botches did him gall,
        Wi' bitter claw,
An' lows'd his ill-tongu'd wicked *Scawl*
        Was warst ava?

But a' your doings to rehearse,
Your wily snares an' fechtin fierce,
Sin' that day MICHAEL did you pierce,
        Down to this time,
Wad ding a' *Lallan* tongue, or *Erse*,
        In Prose or Rhyme.

An' now, auld *Cloots*, I ken ye're thinkan,
A certain *Bardie*'s rantin, drinkin,
Some luckless hour will send him linkan,
          To your black pit;
But faith! he'll turn a corner jinkan,
          An' cheat you yet.

But fare you weel, auld *Nickie-ben*!
O wad ye tak a thought an' men'!
Ye aiblins might—I dinna ken—
          Still hae a *stake*—
I'm wae to think upo' yon den,
          Ev'n for your sake.

S hakespeare is just as adept as Burns when brewing up a vernacular storm, and he too is unshy of showing Death as an experienced hand to be met with on the road. Dr Hornbook is a village quack whose remedies threaten to put the hooded laddie with the scythe out of work, but the real joy here is found in the deployment of vital old Scots words that have now suffered a death themselves in the common speech. Here we have *kittle* ('to excite'), a *spleuchan* ('a skin pouch for tobacco or money') and an *eldritch* laugh – the cackling of elves, which is ghostly, strange, unearthly.

Death and Doctor Hornbook—A True Story

Some books are lies frae end to end,
And some great lies were never penn'd:
Ev'n Ministers they hae been kenn'd,
      In holy rapture,
A rousing whid, at times, to vend,
        And nail't wi' Scripture.

But this that I am gaun to tell,
Which lately on a night befel,
Is just as true's the Deil's in hell,
      Or Dublin city:
That e'er he nearer comes oursel
        'S a muckle pity.

The Clachan yill had made me canty,
I was na fou, but just had plenty;
I stacher'd whyles, but yet took tent ay
      To free the ditches;
An' hillocks, stanes, an' bushes kenn'd ay
        Frae ghaists an' witches.

The rising Moon began to glowr
The distant *Cumnock* hills out-owre;
To count her horns, wi' a' my pow'r,
      I set mysel,
But whether she had three or four,
        I cou'd na tell.

131

I was come round about the hill,
And todlin down on *Willie's mill*,
Setting my staff wi' a' my skill,
              To keep me sicker;
Tho' leeward whyles, against my will,
              I took a bicker.

I there wi' *Something* does forgather,
That pat me in an eerie swither;
An awfu' scythe, out-owre ae shouther,
              Clear-dangling, hang;
A three-tae'd leister on the ither
              Lay, large an' lang.

Its stature seem'd lang Scotch ells twa,
The queerest shape that e'er I saw,
For fient a wame it had ava,
              And then its shanks,
They were as thin, as sharp an' sma'
              As cheeks o' branks.

'Guid-een,' quo' I; 'Friend! hae ye been mawin,
When ither folk are busy sawin?'[1]
I seem'd to mak a kind o' stan',
              But naething spak;
At length, says I, 'Friend, whare ye gaun,
              Will ye go back?'

[1] This encounter happened in seed-time 1785.

It spak right howe—'My name is *Death*,
But be na' fley'd.'—Quoth I, 'Guid faith,
Ye're maybe come to stap my breath;
   But tent me, billie;
I red ye weel, tak care o' skaith,
    See, there's a gully!'

'Gudeman,' quo' he, 'put up your whittle,
I'm no design'd to try its mettle;
But if I did, I wad be kittle
   To be mislear'd,
I wad na' mind it, no that spittle
    Out-owre my beard.'

'Weel, weel!' says I, 'a bargain be't;
Come, gies your hand, an' sae we're gree't;
We'll ease our shanks an' tak a seat,
   Come, gies your news!
This while ye hae been mony a gate,
    At mony a house.'[2]

'Ay, ay!' quo' he, an' shook his head,
'It's e'en a lang, lang time indeed
Sin' I began to nick the thread,
   An' choke the breath:
Folk maun do something for their bread,
    An' sae maun *Death*.

---

[2] An epidemical fever was then raging in that country.

'Sax thousand years are near hand fled
Sin' I was to the butching bred,
And mony a scheme in vain's been laid,
         To stap or scar me;
Till ane Hornbook's³ ta'en up the trade,
         And faith! he'll waur me.

'Ye ken *Jock Hornbook* i' the Clachan,
Deil mak his king's-hood in a spleuchan!
He's grown sae weel acquaint wi' *Buchan*,⁴
         And ither chaps,
The weans haud out their fingers laughin,
         And pouk my hips.

'See, here's a scythe, and there's a dart,
They hae pierc'd mony a gallant heart;
But Doctor *Hornbook*, wi' his art
         And cursed skill,
Has made them baith no worth a fart,
         Damn'd haet they'll kill!

''Twas but yestreen, nae farther gaen,
I threw a noble throw at ane;
Wi' less, I'm sure, I've hundreds slain;
         But deil-ma-care!
It just play'd dirl on the bane,
         But did nae mair.

³ This gentleman, Dr Hornbook, is professionally, a brother of the sovereign Order of the Ferula;
but, by intuition and inspiration, is at once an Apothecary, Surgeon, and Physician.
⁴ Buchan's *Domestic Medicine*.

'*Hornbook* was by, wi' ready art,
And had sae fortify'd the part,
That when I looked to my dart,
      It was sae blunt,
Fient haet o't wad hae pierc'd the heart
      Of a kail-runt.

'I drew my scythe in sic a fury,
I nearhand cowpit wi' my hurry,
But yet the bauld *Apothecary*
      Withstood the shock;
I might as weel hae try'd a quarry
      O' hard whin-rock.

'Ev'n them he canna get attended,
Altho' their face he ne'er had kend it,
Just shit in a kail-blade and send it,
      As soon's he smells't,
Baith their disease, and what will mend it,
      At once he tells't.

'And then a' doctor's saws and whittles,
Of a' dimensions, shapes, an' mettles, .
A' kinds o' boxes, mugs, an' bottles,
      He's sure to hae;
Their Latin names as fast he rattles
      As A B C.

'Calces o' fossils, earths, and trees;
True Sal-marinum o' the seas;
The Farina of beans and pease,
      He has't in plenty;
Aqua-fontis, what you please,
      He can content ye.

'Forbye some new, uncommon weapons,
Urinus Spiritus of capons;
Or Mite-horn shavings, filings, scrapings,
      Distill'd *per se*;
Sal-alkali o' Midge-tail clippings,
      And mony mae.'

'Waes me for *Johnny Ged's-Hole*[5] now,'
Quoth I, 'if that thae news be true!
His braw calf-ward whare gowans grew,
      Sae white an' bonie,
Nae doubt they'll rive it wi' the plew;
      They'll ruin *Johnie*!'

The creature grain'd an eldritch laugh,
And says, 'Ye needna yoke the pleugh,
Kirk-yards will soon be till'd eneugh,
      Tak ye nae fear:
They'll a be trench'd wi' mony a sheugh,
      In twa-three year.

[5] The grave-digger.

'Whare I kill'd ane, a fair strae-death,
By loss o' blood, or want o' breath,
This night I'm free to tak my aith,
      That *Hornbook*'s skill
Has clad a score i' their last claith,
        By drap and pill.

'An honest Wabster to his trade,
Whase wife's twa nieves were scarce weel-bred,
Gat tippence-worth to mend her head,
      When it was sair;
The wife slade cannie to her bed,
       But ne'er spak mair.

'A countra Laird had ta'en the batts,
Or some curmurring in his guts,
His only son for *Hornbook* scts,
      And pays him well,
The lad, for twa guid gimmer-pets,
       Was Laird himsel.

'A bonie lass, ye kend her name,
Some ill-brewn drink had hov'd her wame,
She trusts hersel, to hide the shame,
      In *Hornbook*'s care;
Horn sent her aff to her lang hame,
       To hide it there.

'That's just a swatch o' *Hornbook*'s way,
Thus goes he on from day to day,
Thus does he poison, kill, an' slay,
    An's weel pay'd for't;
Yet stops me o' my lawfu' prey,
    Wi' his damn'd dirt!

'But, hark! I'll tell you of a plot,
Tho' dinna ye be speakin o't;
I'll nail the self-conceited Sot,
    As dead's a herrin:
Neist time we meet, I'll wad a groat,
    He gets his fairin!'

But just as he began to tell,
The auld kirk-hammer strak the bell
Some wee, short hour ayont the *twal*,
    Which rais'd us baith:
I took the way that pleas'd mysel,
    And sae did *Death*.

Burns had the guts to speak of the ways that religion may show itself to be blinded and drowned in a sea of unreason, but all the same he sought heaven for an anchor. I always think of the prime minister, Gordon Brown, when I read the following poem ('May Prudence, Fortitude and Truth/Erect your brow undaunting!'), but since the poem is addressed explicitly to 'Andrew', I grew up thinking it must be meant for me. It is heartening to think that Burns is not above a little Polonius-like hypocrisy, and some of us, in our youth, may have found that perfectly congenial.

Epistle to a Young Friend

I lang hae thought, my youthfu' friend,
  A Something to have sent you,
Tho' it should serve nae other end
  Than just a kind memento;
But how the subject theme may gang,
  Let time and chance determine;
Perhaps it may turn out a Sang;
  Perhaps, turn out a Sermon.

Ye'll try the world soon my lad,
  And ANDREW dear believe me,
Ye'll find mankind an unco squad,
  And muckle they may grieve ye:
For care and trouble set your thought,
  Ev'n when your end's attained;
And a' your views may come to nought,
  Where ev'ry nerve is strained.

I'll no say, men are villains a';
  The real, harden'd wicked,
Wha hae nae check but *human law*,
  Are to a few restricked:
But Och, mankind are unco weak,
  An' little to be trusted;
If *Self* the wavering balance shake,
  It's rarely right adjusted!

Yet they wha fa' in Fortune's strife,
  Their fate we should na censure,
For still th' *important end* of life,
  They equally may answer:
A man may hae an *honest heart*,
  Tho' Poortith hourly stare him;
A man may tak a neebor's part,
  Yet hae nae *cash* to spare him.

Ay free, aff han', your story tell,
  When wi' a bosom crony;
But still keep something to yoursel
  Ye scarcely tell to ony.
Conceal yoursel as weel's ye can
  Frae critical dissection;
But keek thro' ev'ry other man,
  Wi' sharpen'd, sly inspection.

The *sacred lowe* o' weel plac'd love,
  Luxuriantly indulge it;
But never tempt th' *illicit rove*,
  Tho' naething should divulge it:
I wave the quantum o' the sin;
  The hazard of concealing;
But Och! it hardens *a' within*,
  And petrifies the feeling!

To catch Dame Fortune's golden smile,
  Assiduous wait upon her;
And gather gear by ev'ry wile,
  That's justify'd by Honor:
Not for to *hide* it in a *hedge*,
  Nor for a *train-attendant*;
But for the glorious privilege
  Of being *independent*.

The *fear o' Hell*'s a hangman's whip,
  To haud the wretch in order;
But where ye feel your *Honor* grip,
  Let that ay be your border:
Its slightest touches, instant pause—
  Debar a' side-pretences;
And resolutely keep its laws,
  Uncaring consequences.

The great CREATOR to revere,
  Must sure become the *Creature*;
But still the preaching cant forbear,
  And ev'n the rigid feature:
Yet ne'er with Wits prophane to range,
  Be complaisance extended;
An *atheist-laugh*'s a poor exchange
  For *Deity offended*!

When ranting round in Pleasure's ring,
  Religion may be blinded;
Or if she gie a *random-fling*,
  It may be little minded;
But when on Life we're tempest-driven,
  A Conscience but a canker—
A correspondence fix'd wi' Heav'n,
  Is sure a noble *anchor*!

Adieu, dear, amiable Youth!
  Your *heart* can ne'er be wanting!
May Prudence, Fortitude and Truth
  Erect your brow undaunting!
In *ploughman phrase*, 'GOD send you speed,'
  Still daily to grow wiser;
And may ye better reck the *rede*,
  Then ever did th' *Adviser*!

The great night for me in Ayrshire was never Christmas Eve or midsummer, but Halloween, when some sort of folk essence seemed to cling to the cold air. I loved the gathering of nuts and apples door to door, the occasional coins and sweets, while news of immortal bogles and witches travelled abroad in the streets and parks. My mother was very gifted at making costumes, and two of our neighbours, Hazel and Sandy Copeland, who came from the Highlands, threw everything they had into Halloween. At their house we 'dooked' for apples in basins of water and covered our faces in treacle as we tried to take bites from dripping scones that hung on strings from the ceiling. There was always a sense of the warm, excited interior and the frozen world outside, resplendent that night with its dark certainties about the life after death.

The following POEM will, by many Readers, be well enough
understood; but, for the sake of those who are unacquainted
with the manners and traditions of the country where the
scene is cast, Notes are added, to give some account of the
principal Charms and Spells of that Night, so big with
Prophecy to the Peasantry in the West of Scotland. The passion
of prying into Futurity makes a striking part of the history
of Human—nature, in its rude state, in all ages and nations;
and it may be some entertainment to a philosophic mind, if
any such should honor the Author with a perusal, to see the
remains of it, among the more unenlightened in our own.

Halloween[1]

Yes! let the Rich deride, the Proud disdain,
The simple pleasures of the lowly train;
To me more dear, congenial to my heart,
One native charm, than all the gloss of art.

Goldsmith

Upon that *night*, when Fairies light,
  On *Cassilis Downans*[2] dance,
Or owre the lays, in splendid blaze,
  On sprightly coursers prance;

---

[1] Is thought to be a night when Witches, Devils, and other mischief-making beings, are all abroad
on their baneful, midnight errands: particularly, those aerial people, the Fairies, are said, on that
night, to hold a grand Anniversary.
[2] Certain little, romantic, rocky, green hills, in the neighbourhood of the ancient seat of the Earls
of Cassilis.

Or for *Colean,* the rout is taen,
　Beneath the moon's pale beams;
There, up the *Cove,*[3] to stray an' rove,
　Amang the rocks an' streams
　　　　To sport that night.

Amang the bonie, winding banks,
　Where *Doon* rins, wimplin, clear,
Where BRUCE[4] ance rul'd the martial ranks,
　An' shook his *Carrick* spear,
Some merry, friendly, countra folks,
　Together did convene,
To *burn* their nits, an' *pou* their stocks,
　An' haud their *Halloween*
　　　　Fu' blythe that night.

The lasses feat, an' cleanly neat,
  Mair braw than when they're fine;
Their faces blythe, fu' sweetly kythe,
  Hearts leal, an' warm, an' kin':
The lads sae trig, wi' wooer-babs,
  Weel knotted on their garten,
Some unco blate, an' some wi' gabs,
  Gar lasses hearts gang startin
          Whyles fast at night.

Then, first an' foremost, thro' the kail,
  Their *stocks*[5] maun a' be sought ance;
They steek their een, an' grape an' wale,
  For muckle anes, an' straught anes.
Poor hav'rel *Will* fell aff the drift,
  An' wander'd thro' the *Bow-kail*,
An' pow't, for want o' better shift,
  A *runt* was like a sow-tail
          Sae bow't that night.

[5] The first ceremony of Halloween, is, pulling each a *Stock*, or plant of kail. They must go out, hand in hand, with eyes shut, and pull the first they meet with: its being big or little, straight or crooked, is prophetic of the size and shape of the grand object of all their Spells—the husband or wife. If any *yird*, or earth, stick to the root, that is *tocher*, or fortune; and the taste of the *custock*, that is, the heart of the stem, is indicative of the natural temper and disposition. Lastly, the stems, or to give them their ordinary appellation, the *runts*, are placed somewhere above the head of the door; and the christian names of the people whom chance brings into the house, are, according to the priority of placing the *runts*, the names in question.

Then, straught or crooked, yird or nane,
 They roar an' cry a' throw'ther;
The vera *wee-things*, toddlan, rin,
 Wi' stocks out owre their shouther:
An' gif the *custock*'s sweet or sour,
 Wi' joctelegs they taste them;
Syne coziely, aboon the door,
 Wi' cannie care, they've plac'd them
        To lye that night.

The lasses staw frae 'mang them a',
 To pou their *stalks o' corn*;[6]
But *Rab* slips out, an' jinks about,
 Behint the muckle thorn:
He grippet *Nelly* hard an' fast;
 Loud skirl'd a' the lasses;
But her *tap-pickle* maist was lost,
 Whan kiutlan in the *Fause-house*[7]
        Wi' him that night.

---

[6] They go to the barn-yard, and pull each, at three several times, a stalk of Oats. If the third stalk wants the *top-pickle*, that is, the grain at the top of the stalk, the party in question will come to the marriage-bed anything but a Maid.

[7] When the corn is in a doubtful state, by being too green, or wet, the Stack-builder, by means of old timber, &c. makes a large apartment in his stack, with an opening in the side which is fairest exposed to the wind: this he calls a *Fause-house*.

The auld Guidwife's weel-hoordet *nits*[8]
   Are round an' round divided,
An' monie lads an' lasses fates
   Are there that night decided:
Some kindle, couthie, side by side,
   An' *burn* thegither trimly;
Some start awa, wi' saucy pride,
   An' jump out owre the chimlie
            Fu' high that night.

Jean slips in twa, wi' tentie e'e;
   Wha 'twas, she wadna tell;
But this is *Jock*, an' this is *me*,
   She says in to hersel:
He bleez'd owre her, an' she owre him,
   As they wad never mair part,
Till fuff! he started up the lum,
   An' *Jean* had e'en a sair heart
            To see't that night.

Poor *Willie*, wi' his *bow-kail runt*,
   Was *brunt* wi' primsie *Mallie*;
An' *Mary*, nae doubt, took the drunt,
   To be compar'd to *Willie*:
Mall's nit lap out, wi' pridefu' fling,
   An' her ain fit, it brunt it;
While *Willie* lap, an' swoor by *jing*,
   'Twas just the way he wanted
            To be that night.

[8] Burning the nuts is a favourite charm. They name the lad and lass to each particular nut, as they
lay them in the fire; and according as they burn quietly together, or start from beside one another,
the course and issue of the Courtship will be.

Nell had the *Fause-house* in her min',
  She pits hersel an' *Rob* in;
In loving bleeze they sweetly join,
  Till white in ase they're sobbin:
Nell's heart was dancin at the view;
  She whisper'd *Rob* to leuk for't;
Rob, stownlins, prie'd her bonie mou,
  Fu' cozie in the neuk for't,
        Unseen that night.

But *Merran* sat behint their backs,
  Her thoughts on *Andrew Bell*;
She lea'es them gashan at their cracks,
  An' slips out by hersel:
She thro' the yard the nearest taks,
  An' for the *kiln* she goes then,
An' darklins grapet for the *bauks*,
  And in the *blue-clue*[9] throws then,
        Right fear't that night.

[9] Whoever would, with success, try this spell, must strictly observe these directions. Steal out, all alone, to the *kiln*, and, darkling, throw into the *pot*, a clew of blue yarn: wind it in a new clew off the old one; and towards the latter end, something will hold the thread: demand, *wha hauds?* i.e. who holds? and answer will be returned from the kiln-pot, by naming the Christian and sirname of your future Spouse.

An' ay she *win't*, an' ay she swat,
  I wat she made nae jaukin;
Till something *held* within the *pat*,
  Good Lord! but she was quaukin!
But whether 'twas the *Deil* himsel,
  Or whether 'twas a *bauk-en'*,
Or whether it was *Andrew Bell*,
  She did na wait on talkin
          To spier that night.

Wee Jenny to her Graunie says,
  'Will ye go wi' me Graunie?
I'll *eat the apple* at the *glass*,[10]
  I gat frae uncle Johnie:'
She fuff't her pipe wi' sic a lunt,
  In wrath she was sae vap'rin,
She notic't na, an aizle brunt
  Her braw, new, worset apron
          Out thro' that night.

'Ye little Skelpie-limmer's-face!
  I daur you try sic sportin,
As seek the *foul Thief* onie place,
  For him to spae your fortune:
Nae doubt but ye may get a *sight*!
  Great cause ye hae to fear it;
For monie a ane has gotten a fright,
  An' liv'd an' di'd deleeret,
          On sic a night.

---

[10] Take a candle, and go, alone, to a looking glass: eat an apple before it, and some traditions say you should comb your hair all the time: the face of your conjungal companion, *to be*, will be seen in the glass, as if peeping over your shoulder.

'Ae Hairst afore the *Sherra-moor*,
  I mind't as weel's yestreen,
I was a gilpey then, I'm sure,
  I was na past fyfteen:
The Simmer had been cauld an' wat,
  An' *Stuff* was unco green;
An' ay a rantan *Kirn* we gat,
  An' just on *Halloween*
        It fell that night.

'Our *Stibble-rig* was *Rab M'Graen*,
  A clever, sturdy fallow;
His Sin gat *Eppie Sim* wi' wean,
  That liv'd in Achmacalla:
He gat *hemp-seed*,[11] I mind it weel,
  An' he made unco light o't;
But monie a day was *by himsel*,
  He was sae sairly frighted
        That vera night.'

---

[11] Steal out, unperceived, and sow a handful of hemp-seed; harrowing it with any thing you can conveniently draw after you. Repeat, now and then, 'Hemp-seed I saw thee, Hemp-seed I saw thee, and him (or her) that is to be my true-love, come after me and pou thee.' Look over your left shoulder, and you will see the appearance of the person invoked, in the attitude of pulling hemp. Some traditions say, 'come after me and shaw thee,' that is, show thyself; in which case it simply appears. Others omit the harrowing, and say, 'come after me and harrow thee.'

Then up gat fechtan *Jamie Fleck*,
  An' he swoor by his conscience,
That he could *saw hemp-seed* a peck;
  For it was a' but nonsense:
The auld guidman raught down the pock,
  An' out a handfu' gied him;
Syne bad him slip frae 'mang the folk,
  Sometime when nae ane see'd him,
         An' try't that night.

He marches thro' amang the stacks,
  Tho' he was something sturtan;
The *graip* he for a *harrow* taks,
  An' haurls at his curpan:
And ev'ry now an' then, he says,
  'Hemp-seed I saw thee,
An' her that is to be my lass,
  Come after me an' draw thee
         As fast this night.'

He whistl'd up *Lord Lenox' march*,
  To keep his courage cheary;
Altho' his hair began to arch,
  He was sae fley'd an' eerie:
Till presently he hears a squeak,
  An' then a grane an' gruntle;
He by his showther gae a keek,
  An' tumbl'd wi' a wintle
         Out owre that night.

He roar'd a horrid murder-shout,
  In dreadfu' desperation!
An' young an' auld come rinnan out,
  An' hear the sad narration:
He swoor 'twas hilchan *Jean M'Craw*,
  Or crouchie *Merran Humphie*,
Till stop! she trotted thro' them a';
  An' wha was it but *Grumphie*
        Asteer that night?

Meg fain wad to the *Barn* gaen,
  To *winn three wechts o' naething*;[12]
But for to meet the Deil her lane,
  She pat but little faith in:
She gies the Herd a pickle nits,
  An' twa red cheeket apples,
To watch, while for the *Barn* she sets,
  In hopes to see *Tam Kipples*
        That vera night.

[12] This charm must likewise be performed, unperceived and alone. You go to the *barn*, and open both doors; taking them off the hinges, if possible; for there is danger, that the Being, about to appear, may shut the doors, and do you some mischief. Then take that instrument used in winnowing the corn, which, in our country-dialect, we call a *wecht*; and go thro' all the attitudes of letting down corn against the wind. Repeat it three times; and the third time, an apparition will pass thro' the barn, in at the windy door, and out at the other, having both the figure in question and the appearance or retinue, marking the employment or station in life.

She turns the key, wi' cannie thraw,
  An' owre the threshold ventures;
But first on *Sawnie* gies a ca',
  Syne bauldly in she enters:
A *ratton* rattl'd up the wa',
  An' she cry'd, Lord preserve her!
An' ran thro' midden-hole an' a',
  An' pray'd wi' zeal and fervour,
         Fu' fast that night.

They hoy't out Will, wi' sair advice;
  They hecht him some fine braw ane;
It chanc'd the *Stack* he *faddom't thrice*,[13]
  Was timmer-propt for thrawin:
He taks a swirlie, auld *moss-oak*,
  For some black, grousome *Carlin*;
An' loot a winze, an' drew a stroke,
  Till skin in blypes cam haurlin
         Aff's nieves that night.

[13] Take an opportunity of going, unnoticed, to a *Bear-stack*, and fathom it three times round. The last fathom of the last time, you will catch in your arms, the appearance of your future conjugal yoke-fellow.

A wanton widow *Leezie* was,
  As cantie as a kittlen;
But Och! that night, amang the shaws,
  She gat a fearfu' settlin!
She thro' the whins, an' by the cairn,
  An' owre the hill gaed scrievin,
Whare *three Lairds' lan's met at a burn*,[14]
To dip her *left sark-sleeve* in,
          Was bent that night.

Whyles owre a linn the burnie plays,
  As thro' the glen it wimpl't;
Whyles round a rocky scar it strays;
  Whyles in a wiel it dimpl't;
Whyles glitter'd to the nightly rays,
  Wi' bickerin, dancin dazzle;
Whyles cooket underneath the braes,
  Below the spreading hazle
          Unseen that night.

Amang the brachens, on the brae,
  Between her an' the moon,
The Deil, or else an outler Quey,
  Gat up an' gae a croon:
Poor *Leezie*'s heart maist lap the hool;
  Near lav'rock-height she jumpet,
But mist a fit, an' in the *pool*,
  Out owre the lugs she plumpet,
          Wi' a plunge that night.

[14] You go out, one or more, for this is a social spell, to a south-running spring or rivulet, where 'three Lairds' lands meet,' and dip your left shirt-sleeve. Go to bed in sight of a fire, and hang your wet sleeve before it to dry. Ly awake; and sometime near midnight, an apparition, having the exact figure of the grand object in question, will come and turn the sleeve, as if to dry the other side of it.

In order, on the clean hearth-stane,
  The *Luggies*[15] three are ranged;
And ev'ry time great care is taen,
  To see them duely changed:
Auld, uncle *John,* wha *wedlock's joys,*
  Sin' *Mar's-year* did desire,
Because he gat the toom dish thrice,
  He heav'd them on the fire,
        In wrath that night.

Wi' merry sangs, an' friendly cracks,
  I wat they did na weary;
And unco tales, an' funnie jokes,
  Their sports were cheap an' cheary:
Till *buttr'd So'ns,*[16] wi' fragrant lunt,
  Set a' their gabs a steerin;
Syne, wi' a social glass o' strunt,
  They parted aff careerin
        Fu' blythe that night.

---

[15] Take three dishes; put clean water in one, foul water in another, and leave the third empty: blind-fold a person, and lead him to the hearth where the dishes are ranged; he (or she) dips the left hand: if by chance in the clean water, the future husband or wife will come to the bar of Matrimony, a Maid; if in the foul, a widow; if in the empty dish, it foretells, with equal certainty, no marriage at all. It is repeated three times; and every time the arrangement of the dishes is altered.

[16] Sowens, with butter instead of milk to them, is always the *Halloween Supper.*

The Great Author of All Knowledge

The effect of this flight on the public was astonishing, and Lunardi was acclaimed a hero. He must have been suitably flattered at the brisk sale of Lunardi bonnets and Lunardi garters, which the enterprising milliners made and the faster London ladies bought with relish. Perhaps the best tribute to this flight, and to the achievement of aerostation in general, is the inscription still to be read on the monument at Standon: 'Let posterity know, and knowing be astonished, that on the 15th day of September 1784 Vincent Lunardi of Lucca in Tuscany, the First Aerial Traveller in Britain, mounting from the Artillery Ground in London and traversing the Regions of the Air for two Hours and fifteen Minutes, in this spot revisited the Earth. On this rude monument, for ages be recorded that wondrous Enterprise successfully achieved by the Powers of Chemistry and the fortitude of Man, that Improvement in Science which the Great Author of All Knowledge, patronising by His Providence the Invention of Mankind, hath graciously permitted to their Benefit and His own Eternal Glory.'

A History of Flying by C.H. Gibbs-Smith

To a Louse, on Seeing One on a Lady's Bonnet at Church

Ha! whare ye gaun, ye crowlan ferlie!
Your impudence protects you sairly:
I canna say but ye strunt rarely,
      Owre *gawze* and *lace*;
Tho' faith, I fear ye dine but sparely,
      On sic a place.

Ye ugly, creepan, blastet wonner,
Detested, shunn'd, by saunt an' sinner,
How daur ye set your fit upon her,
      Sae fine a *Lady*!
Gae somewhere else and seek your dinner,
      On some poor body.

Swith, in some beggar's haffet squattle;
There ye may creep, and sprawl, and sprattle,
Wi' ither kindred, jumping cattle,
      In shoals and nations;
Whare *horn* nor *bane* ne'er daur unsettle,
      Your thick plantations.

Now haud you there, ye're out o' sight,
Below the fatt'rels, snug and tight,
Na faith ye yet! ye'll no be right,
      Till ye've got on it,
The vera tapmost, towrin height
      O' *Miss's bonnet*.

My sooth! right bauld ye set your nose out,
As plump an' gray as onie grozet:
O for some rank, mercurial rozet,
      Or fell, red smeddum,
I'd gie you sic a hearty dose o't,
      Wad dress your droddum!

I wad na been surpriz'd to spy
You on an auld wife's *flainen toy*;
Or aiblins some bit duddie boy,
      On's *wylecoat*;
But Miss's fine *Lunardi*, fye!
      How daur ye do't?

O *Jenny* dinna toss your head,
An' set your beauties a' abread!
Ye little ken what cursed speed
      The blastie's makin!
Thae *winks* and *finger-ends*, I dread,
      Are notice takin!

O wad some Pow'r the giftie gie us
To see oursels as others see us!
It wad frae monie a blunder free us
      An' foolish notion:
What airs in dress an' gait wad lea'e us,
      An' ev'n Devotion!

The Politics

A noble tradition in Scottish poetry involves the use of animal monologues for comical and political purposes, and Burns sought to advance that tradition in the Kilmarnock edition. His own favourite poet, Robert Fergusson, had used this form in 'The Sow of Feeling' (1773), but Burns must also have been aware of Aesop's blethering dogs and Henryson's *Fables*, as well as Swift's talking horses. We often find these animals can look at human nature as human nature is seldom capable of looking at itself, and the resulting poems, when as well done as this one, are masterpieces of the literary art.

The Death and Dying Words of Poor Mailie, the Author's Only Pet Yowe—An Unco Mournfu' Tale

As Mailie, an' her lambs thegither,
Was ae day nibbling on the tether,
Upon her cloot she coost a hitch,
An' owre she warsl'd in the ditch:
There, groaning, dying, she did ly,
When *Hughoc* he cam doytan by.

Wi' glowrin een, an' lifted han's,
Poor *Hughoc* like a statue stan's;
He saw her days were near hand ended,
But, waes my heart! he could na mend it!
He gaped wide, but naething spak,
At length poor *Mailie* silence brak.

'O thou, whase lamentable face
Appears to mourn my woefu' case!
My *dying words* attentive hear,
An' bear them to my *Master* dear.

'Tell him, if e'er again he keep
As muckle gear as buy a *sheep*,
O, bid him never tye them mair,
Wi' wicked strings o' hemp or hair!
But ca' them out to park or hill,
An' let them wander at their will:
So, may his flock increase an' grow
To *scores* o' lambs, an' *packs* of woo'!

'Tell him, he was a Master kin',
An' ay was guid to me an' mine;
An' now my *dying* charge I gie him,
My helpless *lambs*, I trust them wi' him.

'O, bid him save their harmless lives,
Frae dogs an' tods, an' butchers' knives!
But gie them guid *cow-milk* their fill,
Till they be fit to fend themsel;
An' tent them duely, e'en an' morn,
Wi' taets o' *hay* an' ripps o' *corn*.

'An' may they never learn the gaets,
Of ither vile, wanrestfu' *Pets*!
To slink thro' slaps, an' reave an' steal,
At stacks o' pease, or stocks o' kail.
So may they, like their great *forbears*,
For monie a year come thro' the sheers:
So *wives* will gie them bits o' bread,
An' *bairns* greet for them when they're dead.

'My poor *toop-lamb*, my son an' heir,
O, bid him breed him up wi' care!
An' if he live to be a beast,
To pit some havins in his breast!
An' warn him, what I winna name,
To stay content wi' *yowes* at hame;
An' no to rin an' wear his cloots,
Like ither menseless, graceless brutes.

'An' neist my *yowie*, silly thing,
Gude keep thee frae a *tether string*!
O, may thou ne'er forgather up,
Wi' onie blastet, moorlan *toop*;
But ay keep mind to moop an' mell,
Wi' sheep o' credit like thysel!

'And now, *my bairns*, wi' my last breath,
I lea'e my blessin wi' you baith:
An' when ye think upo' your Mither,
Mind to be kind to ane anither.

'Now, honest *Hughoc*, dinna fail,
To tell my Master a' my tale;
An' bid him burn this cursed *tether*,
An' for thy pains thou'se get my blather.'

This said, poor *Mailie* turn'd her head,
An' clos'd her een amang the dead!

There are also a growing number of larger-scale private enterprises in the Chinese countryside, generating for their owners profits that dwarf by many magnitudes the 'fortunes' for which 'evil landlords' of the old society were submitted to revolutionary justice. Substantial fortunes make it possible, among other things, for some individuals to flaunt population controls by paying the fines for having larger families with impunity; this is among the more serious of the contradictions that rural industry has brought in its wake. Increased polarisation of classes in the rural areas is a serious problem in its own right.

Anthropology and the Global Factory: Studies of the New Industrialization in the Late Twentieth Century, edited by Frances Abrahamer Rothstein and Michael L. Blim

The Twa Dogs—A Tale

'Twas in that place o' *Scotland*'s isle,
That bears the name o' auld king COIL,
Upon a bonie day in June,
When wearing thro' the afternoon,
Twa Dogs, that were na thrang at hame,
Forgather'd ance upon a time.

The first I'll name, they ca'd him *Ceasar*,
Was keepet for His Honor's pleasure;
His hair, his size, his mouth, his lugs,
Show'd he was nane o' Scotland's dogs;
But whalpet some place far abroad,
Whare sailors gang to fish for Cod.

His locked, letter'd, braw brass-collar,
Show'd him the *gentleman* an' *scholar*;
But tho' he was o' high degree,
The fient a pride na pride had he,
But wad hae spent an hour caressan,
Ev'n wi' a' Tinkler-gipsey's *messan*:
At *Kirk* or *Market*, *Mill* or *Smiddie*,
Nae tawtied *tyke*, tho' e'er sae duddie,
But he wad stan't, as glad to see him,
An' stroan't on stanes an' hillocks wi' him.

The tither was a *ploughman's collie*,
A rhyming, ranting, raving billie,
Wha for his friend an' comrade had him,
And in his freaks had *Luath* ca'd him;
After some dog in *Highlan Sang*,
Was made lang syne, lord knows how lang.

He was a gash an' faithfu' *tyke*,
As ever lap a sheugh, or dyke!
His honest sonsie, baws'nt *face*,
Ay gat him friends in ilka place;
His *breast* was white, his towzie *back*,
Weel clad wi' coat o' glossy black;
His gawsie tail, wi' upward curl,
Hung owre his hurdies wi' a swirl.

Nae doubt but they were fain o' ither,
An' unco pack an' thick the gither;
Wi' social *nose* whyles snuff'd an' snowcket;
Whyles mice an' modewurks they howcket;
Whyles scour'd awa in lang excursion,
An' worry'd ither in *diversion*;
Untill wi' daffin weary grown,
Upon a knowe they sat them down,
An' there began a lang digression
About the *lords o' the creation*.

CEASAR

I've aften wonder'd, honest *Luath*,
What sort o' life poor dogs like you have;
An' when the *gentry*'s life I saw,
What way *poor bodies* liv'd ava.

Our *Laird* gets in his racked rents,
His coals, his kane, an' a' his stents;
He rises when he likes himsel;
His flunkies answer at the bell;
He ca's his coach; he ca's his horse;
He draws a bonie, silken purse
As lang's my *tail*, whare thro' the steeks,
The yellow, letter'd *Geordie* keeks.

Frae morn to een, it's nought but toiling,
At baking, roasting, frying, boiling:
An' tho' the gentry first are steghan,
Yet ev'n the *ha' folk* fill their peghan
Wi' sauce, ragouts, an' sic like trashtrie,
That's little short o' downright wastrie.
Our *Whipper-in*, wee, blastiet wonner,
Poor, worthless elf, it eats a dinner,
Better than ony *Tenant-man*
His Honor has in a' the lan':
An' what poor *Cot-folk* pit their painch in,
I own it's past my comprehension.—

LUATH

Trowth, *Ceasar*, whyles they're fash'd eneugh;
A *Cotter* howckan in a sheugh,
Wi' dirty stanes biggan an dyke,
Bairan a quarry, an' sic like,
Himsel, a wife, he thus sustains,
A smytrie o' wee, duddie weans,
An' nought but his han'-daurk, to keep
Them right an' tight in *thack an' raep*.

An' when they meet wi' sair disasters,
Like loss o' health, or want o' masters,
Ye maist wad think, a wee touch langer,
An' they maun starve o' cauld an' hunger:
But how it comes, I never kent yet,
They're maistly wonderfu' contented;
An' buirdly chiels, an' clever hizzies,
Are bred in sic a way as this is.

CEASAR

But then, to see how ye're negleket,
How huff'd, an' cuff'd, an' disrespeket!
Lord man, our gentry care as little
For *delvers*, *ditchers*, an' sic cattle;
They gang as saucy by poor folk,
As I wad by a stinkan brock.

I've notic'd, on our Laird's *court-day*,
An' mony a time my heart's been wae,
Poor *tenant-bodies*, scant o' cash,
How they maun thole a *factor*'s snash;
He'll stamp an' threaten, curse an' swear,
He'll *apprehend* them, *poind* their gear,
While they maun stand, wi' aspect humble,
An' hear it a', an' fear an' tremble!

I see how folk live that hae riches,
But surely poor-folk maun be *wretches*!

LUATH
They're no sae wretched's ane wad think;
Tho' constantly on poortith's brink,
They're sae accustom'd wi' the sight,
The view o't gies them little fright.

Then chance an' fortune are sae guided,
They're ay in less or mair provided;
An' tho' fatigu'd wi' close employment,
A blink o' rest's a sweet enjoyment.

The dearest comfort o' their lives,
Their grushie weans, an' faithfu' wives;
The *prattling things* are just their pride,
That sweetens a' their fire-side.

An' whyles, twalpennie-worth o' *nappy*
Can mak the bodies unco happy;
They lay aside their private cares,
To mind the Kirk an' State affairs;
They'll talk o' *patronage* an' *priests*,
Wi' kindling fury i' their breasts,
Or tell what new taxation's comin,
An' ferlie at the folk in LON'ON.

As bleak-fac'd Hallowmass returns,
They get the jovial, rantan *Kirns*,
When *rural life*, of ev'ry station,
Unite in common recreation;
Love blinks, Wit slaps, an' social Mirth
Forgets there's *care* upo' the earth.

That *merry day* the year begins,
They bar the door on frosty win's;
The nappy reeks wi' mantling ream,
An' sheds a heart-inspiring steam;
The luntan pipe, an' sneeshin mill,
Are handed round wi' right guid will;
The cantie, auld folks, crackan crouse,
The young anes rantan thro' the house—
My heart has been sae fain to see them,
That I for joy hae *barket* wi' them.

Still it's owre true that ye hae said,
Sic game is now owre aften play'd;
There's monie a creditable *stock*
O' decent, honest, fawsont folk,

Are riven out baith root an' branch,
Some rascal's pridefu' greed to quench,
Wha thinks to knit himsel the faster
In favor wi' some *gentle Master*,
Wha, aiblins, thrang a *parliamentin*,
For *Britain's guid* his saul indentin——

CEASAR
  Haith lad, ye little ken about it;
For Britain's guid! guid faith! I doubt it.
Say rather, gaun as PREMIERS lead him,
An' saying *aye* or *no*'s they bid him:
At Operas an' Plays parading,
Mortgaging, gambling, masquerading:
Or maybe, in a frolic daft,
To HAGUE or CALAIS takes a waft,
To make a *tour* an' take a whirl,
To learn *bon ton* an' see the worl'.

  There, at VIENNA or VERSAILLES,
He rives his father's auld entails;
Or by MADRID he takes the rout,
To thrum *guittarres* an' fecht wi' *nowt*;
Or down *Italian Vista* startles,
Whore-hunting amang groves o' myrtles:
Then bowses drumlie *German-water*,
To make himsel look fair an' fatter,
An' clear the consequential sorrows,
Love-gifts of Carnival Signioras.
For Britain's guid! for her destruction!
Wi' dissipation, feud an' faction!

LUATH

Hech man! dear sirs! is that the gate,
They waste sae mony a braw estate!
Are we sae foughten an' harass'd
For gear to gang that gate at last!

O would they stay aback frae courts,
An' please themsels wi' countra sports,
It wad for ev'ry ane be better,
The *Laird*, the *Tenant*, an' the *Cotter*!
For thae frank, rantan, ramblan billies,
Fient haet o' them's illhearted fellows;
Except for breakin o' their timmer,
Or speakin lightly o' their *Limmer*;
Or shootin of a hare or moorcock,
The ne'er-a-bit they're ill to poor folk.

But will ye tell me, Master *Ceasar*,
Sure *great folk*'s life's a life o' pleasure?
Nae cauld nor hunger e'er can steer them,
The vera thought o't need na fear them.

CEASAR

Lord man, were ye but whyles where I am,
The *gentles* ye wad ne'er envy them!

It's true, they needna starve or sweat,
Thro' Winter's cauld, or Summer's heat;
They've nae sair-wark to craze their banes,
An' fill *auld-age* wi' grips an' granes:
But *human-bodies* are sic fools,
For a' their Colledges an' Schools,
That when nae *real* ills perplex them,
They *mak* enow themsels to vex them;
An' ay the less they hae to sturt them,
In like proportion, less will hurt them.

A country fellow at the pleugh,
His *acre's* till'd, he's right eneugh;
A country girl at her wheel,
Her *dizzen's* done, she's unco weel;
But Gentlemen, an' Ladies warst,
Wi' ev'n down *want o' wark* they're curst.
They loiter, lounging, lank an' lazy;
Tho' deil-haet ails them, yet uneasy;
Their days, insipid, dull an' tasteless,
Their nights, unquiet, lang an' restless.

An' ev'n their sports, their balls an' races,
Their galloping thro' public places,
There's sic parade, sic pomp an' art,
The joy can scarcely reach the heart.

The *Men* cast out in *party-matches*,
Then sowther a' in deep debauches.
Ae night, they're mad wi' drink an' whoring,
Niest day their life is past enduring.

The *Ladies* arm-in-arm in clusters,
As great an' gracious a' as sisters;
But hear their *absent thoughts* o' ither,
They're a' run-deils an' jads the gither
Whyles, owre the wee bit cup an' platie,
They sip the *scandal-potion* pretty;
Or lee-lang nights, wi' crabbet leuks,
Pore owre the devil's *pictur'd beuks*;
Stake on a chance a farmer's stackyard,
An' cheat like ony *unhang'd blackguard*.

There's some exceptions, man an' woman;
But this is Gentry's life in common.

By this, the sun was out o' sight,
An' darker gloamin brought the night:
The *bum-clock* humm'd wi' lazy drone,
The kye stood rowtan i' the loan;
When up they gat, an' shook their lugs,
Rejoic'd they were na *men* but *dogs*;
An' each took off his several way,
Resolv'd to meet some ither day.

Might it not be the very model of literary empathy to write so well about a mouse? Burns's pity as well as his creativity was pressed into action after he upset the animal's nest when going about his labours in the field. During his lifetime Burns was often called 'the heaven-taught ploughman', but the glory of the man was to have invented in his writing a heaven on earth, a place where mice and men could share their woes and even extend comfort to each other in the teeth of unknowable fate.

To a Mouse, on Turning Her Up in Her Nest with the Plough, November 1785

Wee, sleeket, cowran, tim'rous *beastie*,
O, what a panic's in thy breastie!
Thou need na start awa sae hasty,
      Wi' bickering brattle!
I wad be laith to rin an' chase thee,
      Wi' murd'ring *pattle*!

I'm truly sorry Man's dominion
Has broken Nature's social union,
An' justifies that ill opinion,
      Which makes thee startle,
At me, thy poor, earth-born companion,
      An' *fellow-mortal*!

I doubt na, whyles, but thou may *thieve*;
What then? poor beastie, thou maun live!
A *daimen-icker* in a *thrave*
      'S a sma' request:
I'll get a blessin wi' the lave,
      An' never miss't!

Thy wee-bit *housie*, too, in ruin!
Its silly wa's the win's are strewin!
An' naething, now, to big a new ane,
      O' foggage green!
An' bleak *December's winds* ensuin,
      Baith snell an' keen!

Thou saw the fields laid bare an' wast,
An' weary *Winter* comin fast,
An' cozie here, beneath the blast,
       Thou thought to dwell,
Till crash! the cruel *coulter* past
        Out thro' thy cell.

That wee-bit heap o' leaves an' stibble,
Has cost thee monie a weary nibble!
Now thou's turn'd out, for a' thy trouble,
       But house or hald,
To thole the Winter's *sleety dribble*,
        An' *cranreuch* cauld!

But, Mousie, thou art no thy-lane,
In proving *foresight* may be vain:
The best laid schemes o' *Mice* an' *Men*,
       Gang aft agley,
An' lea'e us nought but grief an' pain,
        For promis'd joy!

Still, thou art blest, compar'd wi' *me*!
The *present* only toucheth thee:
But Och! I *backward* cast my e'e,
       On prospects drear!
An' *forward*, tho' I canna *see*,
        I *guess* an' *fear*!

Our poet would favour patriotic songs on a night out with fellow Scots, but the sober exciseman and admirer of Addison and Pope could just as easily favour the opposite. Yet his blood could doubtless begin to boil at the mere contemplation both of English wrongs and Scottish complicity. To my mind the following song's greatness is in its hearty encapsulation of a national hobby: wallowing in a chiefly fantastical sense of historical injury. It was already a piece of sentiment by the time Burns wrote it down, but its force is undiminished.

Such a Parcel of Rogues in a Nation

Fareweel to a' our Scotish fame,
  Fareweel our ancient glory;
Fareweel even to the Scotish name,
  Sae fam'd in martial story!
Now Sark rins o'er the Solway sands,
  And Tweed rins to the ocean,
To mark whare England's province stands,
  Such a parcel of rogues in a nation!

What force or guile could not subdue,
  Thro' many warlike ages,
Is wrought now by a coward few,
  For hireling traitors' wages.
The English steel we could disdain,
  Secure in valor's station;
But English gold has been our bane,
  Such a parcel of rogues in a nation!

O would, or I had seen the day
  That treason thus could sell us,
My auld grey head had lien in clay,
  Wi' BRUCE and loyal WALLACE!
But pith and power, till my last hour,
  I'll mak this declaration;
We're bought and sold for English gold,
  Such a parcel of rogues in a nation!

S cotland and England are the only countries in Europe whose national anthems celebrate the defeat of a now benign neighbour, as if that defeat could summon the essence of Scotland, and England too. Burns could also be perfectly rousing in that mode: he hated tyranny in all forms, and in the absence of a real oppressor he could happily reach into the mists of local time and touch on the horrors of proud Edward I, 'the Hammer of the Scots'.

Robert Bruce's March to Bannockburn

Scots, wha hae wi' WALLACE bled,
Scots, wham BRUCE has aften led,
Welcome to your gory bed,——
  Or to victorie.——

Now's the day, and now's the hour;
See the front o' battle lour;
See approach proud EDWARD's power,
  Chains and Slaverie.——

Wha will be a traitor-knave?
Wha can fill a coward's grave?
Wha sae base as be a Slave?
  ——Let him turn and flie:——

Wha for SCOTLAND's king and law,
Freedom's sword will strongly draw,
FREE-MAN stand, or FREE-MAN fa',
  Let him follow me.——

By Oppression's woes and pains!
By your Sons in servile chains!
We will drain our dearest veins,
  But they *shall* be free!

Lay the proud Usurpers low!
Tyrants fall in every foe!
LIBERTY's in every blow!
Let us DO—OR DIE!!!

S cots ballads often work like historical love songs, conjuring lost kings and early graves, giving a simple and personal sound to political woes. They are unforgettable. Burns had a poet's feeling for the Jacobite cause and could make songs that feel as ancient as grief itself. These ballads are part of the weather in Scotland, words blown with the rain, and they echo through the hills like the murmurs of angels.

There'll Never Be Peace till Jamie Comes Hame

By yon castle wa' at the close of the day,
I heard a man sing tho' his head it was grey;
And as he was singing the tears down came,
There'll never be peace till Jamie comes hame.—
The Church is in ruins, the State is in jars,
Delusions, oppressions, and murderous wars:
We dare na weel say't, but we ken wha's to blame,
There'll never be peace till Jamie comes hame.—

My seven braw sons for Jamie drew sword,
And now I greet round their green beds in the yerd;
It brak the sweet heart of my faithfu' auld Dame,
There'll never be peace till Jamie comes hame.—
Now life is a burden that bows me down,
Sin I tint my bairns, and he tint his crown;
But till my last moments my words are the same,
There'll never be peace till Jamie comes hame.—

We could write out this poem, fold it in four, and press it into the breast pockets of Tony Blair and George W. Bush. With Burns's permission, and with something of his zeal for political argument, let us dedicate the poem to the memory of those men and women who will never see Logan Braes again.

There have been 4039 Coalition deaths – 3742 Americans, two Australians, 168 Britons, thirteen Bulgarians, one Czech, seven Danes, two Dutch, two Estonians, one Hungarian, thirty-three Italians, one Kazakh, three Latvians, twenty-one Poles, two Romanians, five Salvadorans, four Slovaks, one South Korean, eleven Spaniards, two Thais and eighteen Ukrainians – in the war in Iraq as of 2 September 2007.

It is estimated that 650,000 Iraqis have died.

Logan Braes

O, Logan, sweetly didst thou glide,
That day I was my Willie's bride;
And years sinsyne hae o'er us run,
Like Logan to the simmer sun.
But now thy flowery banks appear
Like drumlie Winter, dark and drear,
While my dear lad maun face his faes,
Far, far frae me and Logan braes.——

Again the merry month o' May
Has made our hills and vallies gay;
The birds rejoice in leafy bowers,
The bees hum round the breathing flowers:
Blythe Morning lifts his rosy eye,
And Evening's tears are tears of joy:
My soul, delightless, a' surveys,
While Willie's far frae Logan braes.——

Within yon milkwhite hawthorn bush,
Amang her nestlings sits the thrush;
Her faithfu' Mate will share her toil,
Or wi' his song her cares beguile:
But, I wi' my sweet nurslings here,
Nae Mate to help, nae Mate to cheer,
Pass widowed nights and joyless days,
While Willie's far frae Logan braes.——

O wae upon you, Men o' State,
That brethren rouse in deadly hate!
As ye make mony a fond heart mourn,
Sae may it on your heads return!
How can your flinty hearts enjoy
The widow's tears, the orphan's cry:
But soon may Peace bring happy days
And Willie, hame to Logan braes!

Ministry of Defence Press Release

I t is with very deep regret that the Ministry of Defence has to confirm that Fusilier Gordon Campbell Gentle, of Glasgow, was killed in an improvised explosive device attack on British military vehicles in Basra on 28 June 2004. Aged 19, he served with the First Battalion Royal Highland Fusiliers, and was single.

Lieutenant Colonel Paul Cartwright, the Commanding Officer of the First Battalion Royal Highland Fusiliers, said: 'His name says it all. As a new member of the battalion, he settled in with ease, happy in the team environment and always willing to help others. His enthusiasm for his job immediately caught the eye of his peers and superiors alike.' Our thoughts are with his family at this very difficult time.

I Murder Hate

I murder hate by field or flood,
  Tho' glory's name may screen us;
In wars at home I'll spend my blood,
  Life-giving wars of Venus:
The deities that I adore
  Are social Peace and Plenty;
I'm better pleased *to make one more*,
  Than be the death of twenty.—

I would not die like Socrates,
  For all the fuss of Plato;
Nor would I with Leonidas,
  Nor yet would I with Cato:
The Zealots of the Church, or State,
  Shall ne'er my mortal foes be,
But let me have bold ZIMRI's fate,
  Within the arms of COSBI!—

Burns had to conceal his radical sympathies. He didn't always manage this in the public bar, but because of his views, some of his writing, like 'The Tree of Liberty', remained unpublished until forty years after his death. Equality was an obsession: a difficult life had by the end left him hoarse for the virtues of democracy. He admired the Revolution in France, and we may read this poem as evidence of Burns's higher hopes for mankind – his opposition to the wiles of tyranny – while appreciating too how an American-style zeal for 'democracy', in our own day, can threaten to shackle the minds of the people.

The Tree of Liberty

Heard ye o' the tree o' France,
  I watna what's the name o't;
Around it a' the patriots dance,
  Weel Europe kens the fame o't.
It stands where ance the Bastille stood,
  A prison built by kings, man,
When Superstition's hellish brood
  Kept France in leading strings, man.

Upo' this tree there grows sic fruit,
  Its virtues a' can tell, man;
It raises man aboon the brute,
  It maks him ken himsel, man.
Gif ance the peasant taste a bit,
  He's greater than a lord, man,
An' wi' the beggar shares a mite
  O' a' he can afford, man.

This fruit is worth a' Afric's wealth,
  To comfort us 'twas sent, man:
To gie the sweetest blush o' health,
  An' mak us a' content, man.
It clears the een, it cheers the heart,
  Maks high and low gude friends, man;
And he wha acts the traitor's part
  It to perdition sends, man.

My blessings aye attend the chiel
  Wha pitied Gallia's slaves, man,
And staw a branch, spite o' the deil,
  Frae yont the western waves, man.
Fair Virtue water'd it wi' care,
  And now she sees wi' pride, man,
How weel it buds and blossoms there,
  Its branches spreading wide, man.

But vicious folks aye hate to see
  The works o' Virtue thrive, man;
The courtly vermin's banned the tree,
  And grat to see it thrive, man;
King Loui' thought to cut it down,
  When it was unco sma', man;
For this the watchman cracked his crown,
  Cut aff his head and a', man.

A wicked crew syne, on a time,
  Did tak a solemn aith, man,
It ne'er should flourish to its prime,
  I wat they pledged their faith, man.
Awa' they gaed wi' mock parade,
  Like beagles hunting game, man,
But soon grew weary o' the trade
  And wished they'd been at hame, man.

For Freedom, standing by the tree,
  Her sons did loudly ca', man;
She sang a sang o' liberty,
  Which pleased them ane and a', man.
By her inspired, the new-born race
  Soon grew the avenging steel, man;
The hirelings ran—her foes gied chase,
  And banged the despot weel, man.

Let Britain boast her hardy oak,
  Her poplar and her pine, man,
Auld Britain ance could crack her joke,
  And o'er her neighbours shine, man.
But seek the forest round and round,
  And soon 'twill be agreed, man,
That sic a tree can not be found,
  'Twixt London and the Tweed, man.

Without this tree, alake this life
  Is but a vale o' woe, man;
A scene o' sorrow mixed wi' strife,
  Nae real joys we know, man.
We labour soon, we labour late,
  To feed the titled knave, man;
And a' the comfort we're to get
  Is that ayont the grave, man.

Wi' plenty o' sic trees, I trow,
  The warld would live in peace, man;
The sword would help to mak a plough,
  The din o' war wad cease, man.
Like brethren in a common cause,
  We'd on each other smile, man;
And equal rights and equal laws
  Wad gladden every isle, man.

Wae worth the loon wha wadna eat
  Sic halesome dainty cheer, man;
I'd gie my shoon frae aff my feet,
  To taste sic fruit, I swear, man.
Syne let us pray, auld England may
  Sure plant this far-famed tree, man;
And blythe we'll sing, and hail the day
  That gave us liberty, man.

No I'm not going ten thousand miles from home to help murder and burn another poor nation simply to continue the domination of white slave masters of the darker people the world over. This is the day when such evils must come to an end.

Muhammad Ali

The Slave's Lament

It was in sweet Senegal that my foes did me enthrall
  For the lands of Virginia-ginia O;
Torn from that lovely shore, and must never see it more,
  And alas! I am weary, weary O!
   Torn from, &c.

All on that charming coast is no bitter snow and frost,
  Like the lands of Virginia-ginia O;
There streams for ever flow, and there flowers for ever blow,
  And alas! I am weary, weary O!
   There streams, &c.

The burden I must bear, while the cruel scourge I fear,
  In the lands of Virginia-ginia O;
And I think on friends most dear with the bitter, bitter tear,
  And Alas! I am weary, weary O!
   And I think, &c.

Our poet knew that earth was perhaps all the paradise that we shall ever know, and the argument of his days was aimed at restoring the sovereignty of decency and fairness. It was not an ideology or a party, a faction or a government that authored a 'Marseillaise' to the human spirit, but Robert Burns, a farmer's son, who died at 37 with a deep conception of what it means to be alive. His greatest poem is not a farewell to the lasses, the drinks, the immortals or the politics, but a rousing welcome to what is best in each of us, for a' that, as we live and breathe. When the night is over and we make our way home, when the morning is clear and the sky is busy with birds and their songs, we will know our place in the world by the size of our faith in fellowship. It is this conviction which makes Burns the world's greatest and most loveable poet.

A Man's a Man for A' That

Is there, for honest Poverty
  That hings his head, and a' that;
The coward-slave, we pass him by,
  We dare be poor for a' that!
 For a' that, and a' that,
  Our toils obscure, and a' that,
 The rank is but the guinea's stamp,
  The Man's the gowd for a' that.——

What though on hamely fare we dine,
  Wear hoddin grey, and a' that.
Gie fools their silks, and knaves their wine,
  A Man's a Man for a' that.
 For a' that, and a' that,
  Their tinsel show, and a' that;
 The honest man, though e'er sae poor,
  Is king o' men for a' that.——

Ye see yon birkie ca'd a lord,
  Wha struts, and stares, and a' that,
Though hundreds worship at his word,
  He's but a coof for a' that.
 For a' that, and a' that,
  His ribband, star and a' that,
 The man of independent mind,
  He looks and laughs at a' that.——

A prince can mak a belted knight,
    A marquis, duke, and a' that;
But an honest man's aboon his might,
    Gude faith he mauna fa' that!
  For a' that, and a' that,
    Their dignities, and a' that,
  The pith o' Sense, and pride o' Worth,
    Are higher rank than a' that.—

Then let us pray that come it may,
    As come it will for a' that,
That Sense and Worth, o'er a' the earth
    Shall bear the gree, and a' that.
  For a' that, and a' that,
    It's comin yet for a' that,
  That Man to Man the warld o'er,
    Shall brothers be for a' that.—

Glossary

A

aft often
agley wrong
aiblins perhaps
aidle ditch water
airn iron
airt direction
aits oats
aizle ember
aqua-fontis spring water
aquavitae whisky
ase ashes
asklent askew
asteer abroad
auldfarran sagacious, shrewd
aumous alms
ava at all
awnie bearded
ayont past

B

bair clear
bairn child
bakes biscuits
barley-bree whisky
batts colic
bauk cross-beam; **bauk-en'**
    end of a cross-beam
baws'nt brindled
bear barley
bear the gree come off best
benmost furthest in
bestead placed
bicker wooden drinking vessel
bicker stagger; rush
bide endure
bield shelter
bienly comfortably
big build
bill bull
billie fellow
birk birch
birkie lively fellow
bizz flurry
blastet cursed; **blastie** nasty
    creature
blate bashful

blather bladder

bleeze blaze

blellum blusterer

blether talk foolishly

blink look fondly

blinker spy, cheat

blype layer

boddle copper coin

boortree elder

bore crevice

botch tumour

bow-kail cabbage

branks halter, bridle

brash sudden illness

brats rags

brattle hurry

braw handsome; **brawlie** admirably

bree whisky

brock badger

brogue trick

brunstane brimstone

budget leather bag

buirdly stalwart

bum hum; **bum-clock** humming beetle

burn stream

burnewin blacksmith

butt and ben everywhere

byke hive; crowd

C

ca'd hammered

cadger travelling hawker

cadie rascal

caff chaff

caird tinker

calces powders

calf-ward churchyard

callet wench

callor fresh

cannie pleasant

cantie, canty cheerful, lively

cantraip magic

carlin witch; old fellow

cattle beasts

cavie coop

change-house ale-house

chap stroke

chapman pedlar

cheek-for-chow cheek by jowl

cheeks side-pieces

chiel fellow

chuck sweetheart

chuffie portly, fat faced

clachan village

clash gossip

clatter chatter, gossip

claw scratching

cleek   link hands in a dance; steal; **claught** clutched

clew, clue   ball of yarn

clink   sit down smartly

cloot   hoof; **Cloots** the devil

clout   cloth; patch

coff   buy

cog   wooden drinking vessel

coof   lout, fool

cook   dart in and out of sight

coost   looped

cootie   tub

core   band of dancers, party

cot   cottage; **cotter** cottager, tenant farmer

cour   fold

court-day   rent-day

couthie   loving

cowe   scold, berate

cowp   fell over

crack   gossip, story

craigie   throat

crank   harsh sound

cranreuch   hoar-frost

creeshie   greasy, filthy

croose, crouse   cocksure, merry

crouchie   hump-backed

crowdie-time   breakfast time

crummock   short staff with a crooked head

crump   baked dry

curmurring   rumbling

curpan   backside

custock   kale-stalk

cutty   short

D

daffin   flirtation, fooling

dail   plank

daimem-icker   occasional ear of corn

damn'd haet   damn all

daunton   cast down

daut   pet, make much of; **dawtit** spoiled

dawd   hunk

deil-haet   nothing; **deil-mak-matter** no matter

delver   gardener, labourer

dight   wipe dry; winnow

ding   overcome

dint   occasion

dirk, durk   short Highland dagger

dirl   shake

dizzen   work amounting to a day's spinning

doited   enfeebled; **doytan** blundering

donsie   hapless

dorty   haughty

douce, douse sedate

douk duck

dow be able

doylt muddled

driddle dawdle

droddum backside

drouth thirst

drumlie cloudy; gloomy

drunt sulks

dub stagnant pool, puddle

dud(d)ies, duds clothes;
  duddie ragged

dung in beaten into

E

eldritch uncanny,
  frightful

Erse Gaelic

ettle purpose

F

fa' befall

fain glad; **fain o' ither** fond of
  each other

fairin deserts

faith ye confound ye

fash trouble; **fash your thumb**
  pay heed

fatt'rels ribbon ends

fawsont respectable

feat trim

feck most

fell powerful

Ferintosh a brand of whisky,
  exempted from duty in repara-
  tion for the damage done to the
  estates of Forbes of Culloden,
  the distillery's owner, by the
  Jacobites in 1689. The loss of
  the exemption in 1785 drove
  up the price of whisky.

ferlie wonder

fidge shrug; **fidge fu' fain**
  twitch with excitement

fient haet nothing

fiere companion

fit(t) foot

fley terrify

foggage rank grass, winter
  grazing

forbye besides

fou, fu' drunk; very

foughten harassed, worn out

freak fancy

free clear

fud backside

fuff puff

funny merry

furr furrow

fyke commotion

G

gab mouth

gaets habits

gangrel tramp

gar make, cause

gash chat; neat; shrewd

gate way

gausy, gawsie fine; plump

gear possessions, property

gentles gentry

Geordie guinea

gilpey young girl

gimmer-pet yearling ewe kept as a pet

gin before

girdle griddle

gizz wig

glaikit foolish

gloaming twilight

glowr gaze intently

glunch scowl

gowan daisy

gowd gold

graip garden fork

graith ploughing gear; habit

greet cry

grozet gooseberry

grumphie sow

gruntle nose; grunt

grushie thriving

gude-willie-waught generous draught

gully large knife

gusty tasty

gutscraper fiddler

H

ha' folk servants

haffet temple

hafflins-wise nearly

hairst harvest

hald refuge

han'-daurk manual labour

harn coarse linen

hash waster

haugh level, fertile land by a river

haurl drag; peel

havins good manners

hav'rel half-wit

hawkie cow with a white face

hecht promise

herd herd-boy

heugh pit

hilch limp

hirple limp; move unevenly

hizzie whore; silly girl

hoast cough

hoddan bumping up and down in the saddle

hoddin coarse grey homespun cloth

Hornie the devil

hotch jerk about

houghmagandie sex

houlet owl(et)

hove make swell

howck dig up

howdie midwife

howe hollow

hoy't urged on

huff scold

hum take in

hurchin urchin

hurdies haunches

I

ilka each, every

J

jad woman; hussy

jaukin delay

jink dodge

jo sweetheart

jocteleg clasp-knife

jow toll

K

kae thief

kail-runt stalk of the kail plant

kane payment in kind

kebar rafter

kebbuck homemade cheese

keek peek

kennin little

kings'-hood paunch

kintra country

kirn merrymaking at the end of harvest; churn

kittle tune up, play; rouse

kiutle fondle, cuddle

kye cows

kythe make known

L

lane lonely; **her lane** by herself; **thy-lane** by yourself

lave rest

lav'rock lark

lay, lea pasture

leal loyal

lear learning

lee lang whole

leeze me a blessing on

leister trident

lift sky

limmer mistress

link skip

list enlist

loan milking place

loot let out

lowe rage, blaze

lowp leap; **lap** leapt; **lap the hool** jumped out of her chest

lugget caup shallow wooden dish with handles; **luggie** wooden dish

lunt puff of smoke; steam

lyart streaked red and white; grey

M

Mahoun the devil

mailin smallholding, tenant farm

man of Uzz Job

Mar's-year 1715, when the Earl of Mar led the Jacobite revolt

mashlum mixed meal

meikle, muckle great; **meikle corn** oats

melder an occasion when a customer's corn was taken to be ground at the mill

mell have dealings with

melvie soil

men' repent

menseless boorish

messan lap-dog; cur

midden-hole hole in a dung heap

mim demure

mirk dark

mischanter mishap

mislear'd mischievous

mite-horn horn on the harvest-bug

modewurk mole

moop nibble

muscle mussel

N

nappy ale

nieve fist

niffer comparison

noddle head

norland northern

O

o' boot as well

orra spare

outler quey young cow lying out at night

P

pack intimate

pang stuff

party-match card competition

pattle, pettle spade used to clean the plough

peghan stomach
penny-wheep small beer
philibeg kilt
pictur'd beuks playing cards
plack small coin; **plackless** penniless
plaidie tartan cloak
pliskie trick
pliver green plover
plumpet sank
pock bag
poortith poverty
pou, pow, pu pull
press cupboard
prie her mou' kiss her
pussie hare
pyke pick at
pyle grain

Q

quean young girl
queir choir

R

raible gabble
rak'd her had sex with her
randie rude, riotous
rant spree; **rantan** merry
rape rope

rash-buss clump of rushes
ratton rat
raucle rough, coarse
raught reached
ream foam
reave thieve
reck heed
rede advice
reekan bloody; **reeket** smoky
reestet cured
remead remedy
rigwoodie withered
ripp handful
rive break up
roose praise
roupet husky
row roll
rowte low
rowth plenty
rozet resin
run-deil complete devil
rung cudgel
runkl'd wrinkled
runt cabbage stalk
ryke reach

S

sair-wark labour
sark shift; **sark-neck** collar

scaur afraid

scrieve glide swiftly

settlin quieting

shavie trick

shaw small wood in a hollow

sheugh trench

shore offer; threaten

sicker steady

sinsyne since then

skaith damage

skellum rascal

skelpie-limmer hussy; **skelp** slap; hurry; **skelpan, skelping** smacking

skirl shriek

sklent direct with malice; slanting

skyte blow that rebounds at an angle

slae blackthorn

slap gap in a dyke or fence

sleeket smooth

smeddum insecticide powder

smoor'd was smothered

smoutie ugly

smytrie numerous collection

snash abuse

sneeshin mill snuff box

snell bitter

snick-drawing crafty

snirtle snigger

snowck sniff

sonsie good-natured

souple soft

sowther patch up

spae foretell

spairge bespatter

span-lang hand's-breadth

spean wean

spier ask

spleuchan tobacco pouch, purse

splore uproar

sprattle scramble

spunkie will o' the wisp

stan' pause

stank pond

staw stole

steek stitch

steek shut

steer molest

(a) steerin in motion

stegh stuff oneself with food

stent duty

stibble-rig reaper who takes the lead

stirk young bullock

stoiter stagger

stoor harsh

stoure tumult

stowlins stealthily

stowp tankard

strae–death natural death in bed

streek stretch

stroan't pissed

strunt liquor

strunt move confidently, strut

studdie anvil

sturt trouble; **sturtan** afraid

sucker sugar

sugh rushing sound of wind

swat sweated

swats new small beer

swirlie full of knots

swither state of agitated uncertainty

syne then; **lang syne** long ago

T

tack tenure

taet tuft

tak aff drink up; **tak the gate** go home

tap-pickle grain at the end of the stalk

tapsalteerie topsy-turvy

tassie goblet

tawtied shaggy

tent open-air pulpit

tent care; take heed; **tentie** watchful

thack thatch

thairms fiddle strings

thole endure

thrang crowd; in a crowd, busy

thrave two sets of corn sheaves

thraw frustrate; twist; **for thrawing** to prevent warping

(a') throu'ther, throw'ther in confusion

till't to it

timmer timber

tine lose

tippeny ale originally sold at 2d a Scots pint

tirl rattle

tod fox

toom empty

toop ram

tow bell-rope

towsing fondling

towzie unkempt, shaggy

toy old-fashioned cap

tozie tipsy

trepan beguile

trig smart
trow believe
tryst cattle market
twin deprive

U

unco very; strange
usquabae, usquebae whisky

V

vap'rin fuming
vauntie vain

W

wabster weaver
wae sucks alas; **wae worth** cursed be
waft sea-trip
wale choicest kind; choose, pick out
wame stomach; womb
warklum tool
warsle struggle
wat know, be sure
water-fit mouth of a river
waver flutter
wawlie fine, handsome
wean child
weary fa' a curse on

weason gullet
whang thick slice of cheese
whid lie
whiles, whyles at times
whin gorse
whitter draught of liquor
whittle knife
wiel eddy
wight fellow
wimple twist, meander
winn winnow
winnock window; **winnock-bunker** window-seat
win't wound
wintle roll
winze curse
wonner specimen
woodie rope for hanging
wooer-bab garter at knee tied with two loops and worn by a suitor
worms long spiral tubes at the head of a whisky still in which the vapour is condensed
worset worsted
wud angry
wyle lure
wylecoat flannel vest
wyte reproach

Y

yell milkless

yill ale; **yill-caup** wooden vessel for drinking ale

yird earth

Acknowledgments

The idea for this book was Jamie Byng's and was executed with flair by Anya Serota. We wanted to make a reader's selection of the greatest poems and we relied on the notion that Robert Burns, perhaps more than any other great poet, might suffer to be entertained by some personal camaraderie in the company of a junior writer of prose. Thanks are due to everyone at Canongate and to my friends Karl Miller and Seamus Heaney, to earlier editors James Kinsley, Andrew Noble, Patrick Scott Hogg and Carol McGuirk, whose own editions helped me along the way, and to another friend, Jean McNicol, who edited the manuscript with fantastic care and imagination. I thank each of them for their cups of kindness and for helping me to arrange a night out with Robert Burns that might leave us drunk but unbleary.

Andrew O'Hagan
London, March 2007